Aunty A's
Big Island Eats

Favorite Island Recipes from Chefs, Restaurants, and Community Members

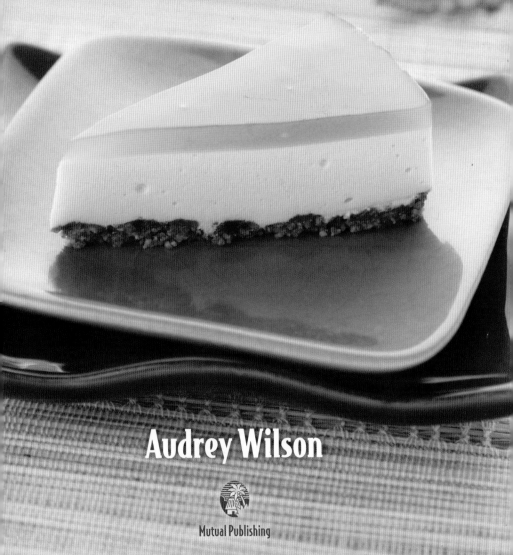

Audrey Wilson

Mutual Publishing

Library of Congress Cataloging-in-Publication Data

Wilson, Audrey.
  Aunty Audrey's Big Island eats / Audrey Wilson.
    p. cm.
  Includes index.
  ISBN 1-56647-928-2 (softcover : alk. paper)
  1. Hawaiian cookery. 2. Cooking--Hawaii--Hawaii Island. I. Title. II. Title: Big Island eats.
  TX724.5.H3W534 2010
  641.59969--dc22
                  2010025663

ISBN-10: 1-56647-928-2
ISBN-13: 978-1-56647-928-8

Design by Courtney Young
Full-page food photography by Kaz Tanabe; also photos on pg. 3, 7-9, 15, 18, 26, 39, 41, 52, 55, 57, 67, 74, 84, 97, 101, 116 (bottom photo), 157, 212, 229, 240 (author photo)
Photo of Chef Alan Wong on pg. 43 © Mary Ann Changg
Photo on pg. 13 © KTA Super Stores
Photo on pg. 108 © Hilo Coffee Mill and Jim Wilson
Photo on pg. 128 © Mitsuo Takaki
Photos on pg. 132-134 © Audrey Wilson
Photo on pg. 186 © Sachi Ogawa
Photo of Chef Mark Tsuchiyama on pg. 187 © Kona Village PR firm
Unless otherwise noted, all other photographs © Jim Wilson
The following spot photograhs from dreamstime.com
    pg. 12 © Andrzej Tokarski, pg. 62 © Sierpniowka, pg. 113 © Chiyacat

First Printing, September 2010

Mutual Publishing, LLC
1215 Center Street, Suite 210
Honolulu, Hawai'i 96816
Ph: 808-732-1709 / Fax: 808-734-4094
email: info@mutualpublishing.com
www.mutualpublishing.com

Printed in Korea

Table of Contents

COMMUNITY FAVORITES

RESTAURANTS OF THE BIG ISLAND

CELEBRATIONS, FESTIVALS, AND LŪʻAU

MEMORIES OF THE PAST

OMIYAGE SWEETS

Acknowledgments

MAHALO TO:

Barry Taniguchi, CEO of KTA Super Stores, for sponsoring this book.

Jack K. Fujii, retired dean of the University of Hawai'i at Hilo, College of Agriculture, for compiling his wonderful cookbooks, such as *Focus on Agriculture: Recipes from the Big Island of Hawai'i.*

Jim D. Wilson, retired publisher of the *Hawai'i Tribune Herald* and also my husband, for driving me here, there, and everywhere, and for taking countless photos. Taking pictures was a new experience for him, but he took them until he was satisfied with his photos. This was real "on-the-job" training—and I'm thrilled with the results. Thanks for your patience, Jim.

KTA 'Ohana

All of the recipes in this section were contributed by members of the KTA 'ohana—a group that includes not only the Taniguchi family, but the employees of the store.

KTA Super Stores is now one the largest employers on the Big Island; it runs five supermarkets here. It has also been an enthusiastic supporter of local agriculture and local companies, buying local produce and introducing its line of Mountain Apple products—hundreds of tasty foods unique to the Big Island. Many of the recipes in this book use Mountain Apple products and KTA's local produce.

KTA started out in 1916 as a family company, a small store run by Koichi and Taniyo Taniguchi in Waiākea. Hard work and great customer service paid off for the Taniguchis. Their small store is now a supermarket chain. Their grandchildren and great-grandchildren are still actively involved in the management of the store.

Of course, they had to hire outside the Taniguchi family as they expanded ... but KTA has always cherished that Island 'ohana feeling. I have had the pleasure of meeting many of the KTA employees, and I have always been impressed by their cheerful esprit de corps.

The KTA 'ohana were generous in sharing recipes with me—and with you. They work with food all day; they know good food; they like to cook good food. Because they are hardworking folks, they are also fond of quick-and-easy recipes made with products that they can pick up at the store just before they head home. I believe that you'll find their recipes a useful addition to your list of surefire, last-minute dishes.

"Serving you since 1916"

Kūlolo

Kūlolo, or taro pudding, is usually available at KTA Super Stores, at the seafood counter. KTA kūlolo is made by Puʻueo Poi, a Big Island company.

If you have some taro and want to make your own kūlolo, here is an easy recipe. Do remember that raw taro contains crystals of calcium oxalate, which can irritate the skin. Boil the taro before peeling and grating it.

INGREDIENTS:
4 cups grated taro root
¾ cup brown sugar
1 cup Hawaiian honey
1 cup coconut milk
2 ti leaves

PREPARATION:

Scrub the taro roots with a vegetable brush, put them in a large pot, and cover with water. Boil until thoroughly cooked. Test with a kitchen knife or a fork to be sure.

Peel and grate the roots. Measure out 4 cups. Excess taro can be frozen for later use.

Mix the grated taro, brown sugar, honey, and coconut milk.

Line a loaf pan with foil. Cut the ti leaves to fit the pan and place the ti leaves on the foil. Pour the taro mixture into the pan and cover with foil. Bake at 400°F for 2 hours. Remove the foil cover during the last half hour to allow the pudding to brown.

PRESENTATION:

Kūlolo is best eaten soon after it is made. If you store it in the refrigerator, it will become hard and dry.

Baking a Cake in a Soda Box
SERVES 12

Derek Kurisu is the *marketing guy at KTA Super Stores. Derek made this cake for Governor Linda Lingle. She certainly enjoyed it!*

INGREDIENTS:
   1 cardboard box used to hold 6 cans of soda
   Parchment paper
   2 (18.25 ounce) boxes Betty Crocker SuperMoist cake mix
   2½ cups water
   1 cup (2 sticks) butter, softened
   6 large eggs

PREPARATION:
Preheat the oven to 350°F.

Prepare the soda box by lining the sides and bottom with parchment paper. Use two long strips of paper. Do not use any tape to hold the paper; you don't want the chemicals in the tape to seep into your cake.

Put the cake mix, water, butter, and eggs in a bowl and mix well.

Pour the cake batter into the prepared soda box and spread evenly.

Bake for 32 to 37 minutes, insert toothpick in center and be sure if come out clean.

Cool and add frosting.

Salmon with Mountain Apple Guava Sauce
SERVES 6

This recipe makes excellent use of Mountain Apple Guava Sauce. It is best made with a mix of red, green, and yellow peppers. If you can't find or afford all three varieties, you can just use the common green peppers. The dish won't be as colorful or flavorful, but it will still be tasty.

INGREDIENTS:
2 pounds salmon fillet
1 (12 ounce) bottle Mountain Apple Guava Sauce, found in the refrigerated meat section
1 large egg, beaten
¼ cup all-purpose flour
3 tablespoons olive oil
2 cups mixed peppers, red, green, and yellow (about ½ each of 3
medium-size peppers)
½ cup fresh shiitake mushroom, julienne

PREPARATION:
Pour the guava sauce over the salmon fillet and refrigerate the salmon, covered, overnight.

The next day, beat the egg in a small bowl or pan. Measure the flour into an-other pan. Remove the stem, seeds, and white membrane from the peppers, and cut them into julienne strips. Cut the mushrooms into slices and then into julienne strips.

Put 2 tablespoons of the olive oil in a frying pan and turn the heat to medium-high. When the oil is hot (you can hold your hand above the oil to feel the heat), remove the fish from the guava marinade and dip it in the beaten egg, then dip it in the flour to coat. Fry the salmon in the olive oil for approximately 3 minutes on each side. Place the cooked salmon on a platter.

Pour the rest of the olive oil into the pan and quickly sauté the bell peppers and shiitake mushrooms. This should take only 5 to 7 minutes; do not over-cook. Add the reserved guava sauce and simmer the mixtures for another 7 to 10 minutes.

Pour the pepper-mushroom sauce over the salmon and serve.

Watercress Chicken Salad
SERVES 6 TO 8

Mountain Apple watercress is the one of the main ingredients in this great salad. If you already have some cooked chicken on hand, you can easily put together this main-dish salad. Try this for supper on a hot and humid day.

INGREDIENTS:

For the hoisin vinaigrette:
2 (3-inch) pieces fresh Big Island ginger, peeled and thinly sliced
2 medium-size stalks of green onion, coarsely chopped
½ cup hoisin sauce
¼ cup rice vinegar
2 tablespoons water
¼ cup canola oil
1 tablespoon sesame oil
Salt and pepper to taste

For the salad:
2 bunches (approximately 10 ounces) Mountain Apple watercress
8 cups cooked chicken, shredded (requires approximately 2 pounds of raw chicken; use breasts and thighs for easier cooking and shredding)
4 cups bell peppers, julienne (approximately 1 each medium-size green, red, and yellow bell pepper [or 3 green bell peppers, if less expensive or more readily available])

PREPARATION:

To prepare the vinaigrette: Peel and finely chop the ginger. Trim and roughly chop 1 stalk of green onion. Put the ginger and green onion in a food processor. Add the hoisin sauce, rice vinegar, water, oil, and sesame oil, and blend until smooth. Season to taste with salt and pepper.

To prepare the chicken: Boil enough water or chicken broth to cover the chicken. Lower the heat to a simmer and add the chicken. Cook for 15 to 20 minutes if you are using cut-up chicken; a whole chicken may take 45 minutes or more. Pull out a piece of the chicken and test to be sure that it is thoroughly cooked before removing and draining the chicken. Of course, you shouldn't go to the other extreme and overcook the chicken; you want it to be moist and tender, not dry and hard to chew. Let it cool before you shred it.

(I like poached chicken for chicken salads, but you can use leftover baked chicken if that's what you have.)

Once you've shredded the cooked chicken, measure out the 8 cups you'll need for this recipe. Any extra can be frozen and used in many other dishes.

Prepare the peppers: Wash, remove stems, seeds, and the white inner membranes and cut into julienne strips no wider than ⅛-inch.

Wash the watercress. Wash, trim and finely slice the remaining green onion.

PRESENTATION:

Arrange the washed watercress on a serving platter. Combine the shredded chicken and bell pepper slices in a large mixing bowl. Arrange the chicken and pepper in a large mound on the watercress. Drizzle the dressing generously over the salad. Sprinkle the salad with the remaining green onion. Serve immediately.

Portuguese Kale Soup
SERVES 8 TO 10

Tony Armstrong, front-end supervisor at KTA Super Stores, learned to make this soup from his grandmother. This soup is a traditional healthy treat, packed with vitamins and minerals.

The perfect soup will feature tender beef and crisp vegetables in a thin broth. The broth should be watery, not thick like split-pea soup. The split peas are only there to add a little extra color and flavor. If you add too many peas and the soup is too thick, thin with water. The beef shank should be cooked till it is falling-off-the-fork tender; the vegetables should still have some texture and crunch.

Don't add any black pepper to the soup. The Portuguese sausage is spicy, and that's enough!

INGREDIENTS:
- 4 quarts water
- 1 to 2 tablespoons salt, to taste
- ½ cup dried split green peas
- 2 large beef shanks (approximately 1½ pounds)
- 3 (10 ounce) Portuguese sausages
- 2 bunches kale or collard greens
- 1 medium-size head cabbage
- 1 medium-size onion, coarsely chopped into 1-inch pieces
- ¼ cup fresh mint or spinach, chopped
- 3 large potatoes

PREPARATION:

Some cooks like to trim extra fat and gristle from the beef shanks; some use the shanks as is. You can do as you please here.

Pour the 4 quarts of water into a large pot and add salt to taste. Add the split green peas, and beef shanks. Cook the peas and beef on medium to medium-high heat until tender, approximately 1 to 2 hours.

Remove the beef shanks and set them aside in a covered pot or bowl.

Wash the kale, trim any discolored stems, and chop into pieces at least 1-inch wide and long; if the kale is chopped too finely, the soup won't have enough texture. Add the kale to the soup pot with the split peas and beef broth. Cook the soup until the kale begins to soften, about ½ hour.

While the soup is cooking, core and quarter the cabbage. Cut it into 1-inch pieces. Cut the onion into chunks 1-inch or smaller. If using mint, wash, remove the leaves from the stalks, and chop coarsely. If using spinach, wash thoroughly, re-move any tough stems, and chop coarsely. Peel the potatoes and cut into 1-inch cubes.

Add the cabbage, onion, mint or spinach, and potato to the soup. Cook for an-other half hour, or less. Do not over-cook the potatoes or they will disintegrate.

While the vegetables are cooking, chop the Portuguese sausage into slices no more than ½-inch thick. Cut the reserved beef shank into 1-inch chunks.

Turn off the stove and let soup sit for about 10 minutes before serving. This rest-ing period lets the flavors in the soup mix, as well as making sure that the soup isn't too hot to eat.

If you are going to serve the soup family-style, you can mix the sausage and beef into the soup at this point. If you plan individual servings, leave them aside.

PRESENTATION:

For individual servings, put a layer of sausage and beef shank into the bottom of individual bowls, then ladle soup into the bowls. For a family-style presentation, put soup, sausage, and beef into a large serving bowl or tureen.

Tony likes to serve this soup with thick slices of buttered Portuguese sweet bread. Dunk the bread into the soup and savor the delicious contrasts of flavor and texture.

Salami Salad
with Tomatoes and Mozzarella
SERVES 8

Merle Unoki buys the gourmet and deli foods for KTA Super Stores. She likes to experiment with the deli foods; they're a quick-and-easy shortcut to a healthy dinner after a hard day's work. Here is one of her favorite recipes, made with salami and mozzarella from the deli.

INGREDIENTS:
1 pound salami, cut into ¼-inch cubes or chunks
6 medium-size Big Island tomatoes, cut into ½-inch dice
½ cup fresh Big Island basil leaves
½ pound mozzarella, cut into ½-inch pieces
Salt and freshly ground black pepper
Extra virgin olive oil, for drizzling
Balsamic vinegar, for drizzling

PREPARATION:

It will take just a few minutes to wash and chop the tomatoes and basil, and to cut up the salami and mozzarella.

Combine the salami, tomatoes, basil, and mozzarella in a large bowl. Season to taste with salt and pepper. Drizzle with extra virgin olive oil and vinegar and toss well.

1/8/2011 Mahalo party

Asian Spiced Eggplant Spread
SERVES 10

Here is a tasty Asian-flavored spread from Buyer Merle Unoki. Serve it with crudités, crackers, or slices of crusty French bread.

INGREDIENTS:

1 tablespoon sesame seeds
2 medium eggplants (round, not Oriental)
2 tablespoons olive oil
1 garlic clove, peeled, smashed with the flat side of your chef's knife
1 (1-inch) piece of fresh ginger, peeled and sliced
1 stalk green onion, washed, trimmed, and cut into 2-inch pieces
2 tablespoons soy sauce
2 tablespoons rice vinegar
1 tablespoon sugar
1 teaspoon sesame oil
½ to 1 teaspoon crushed red pepper flakes, to taste
½ teaspoon salt
¾ cup cilantro leaves, trimmed and washed

PREPARATION:

Preheat the oven to 450°F. While the oven is heating, toast the sesame seeds in a small dry frying pan over low heat, stirring constantly, until they are golden and fragrant; this will take about 5 minutes. Set the sesame seeds aside.

Scrub the eggplants and cut off the stems, but don't peel them. Slice them into ¼-inch thick pieces.

Lightly oil 2 baking sheets and arrange the eggplant slices on the sheets, in a single layer. Lightly brush both sides of each slice with a little olive oil. Slide the sheets into the pre-heated oven and bake for 30 to 35 minutes, or until the eggplant slices are fork-tender. Don't turn the slices.

While the eggplant is baking, you can peel and smash the garlic, peel and slice the ginger, clean and chop the green onion, and trim and wash the cilantro leaves.

Remove the full-cooked eggplant, let it cool, then chop it coarsely.

When all the ingredients are ready, turn on your food processor and feed the garlic, ginger, and green onion into the chute. When they are minced, add the roasted eggplant, soy sauce, vinegar, sugar, sesame oil, crushed red pepper flakes, salt, and pepper. Add half of the cilantro leaves. Purée till smooth.

PRESENTATION:

Spoon the spread into a serving dish and garnish with the remaining cilantro and the toasted sesame seeds.

1/8/2011 Mahalo Party
9/2016 Megan Misuda baby shower

Tex-Mex Taco Dinner
SERVES 4

Nicole Onishi shared this recipe with me. She is the granddaughter of Tony Taniguchi, son of Koichi and Taniyo Taniguchi, founders of KTA Super Stores. This is one of her favorite dishes. It's so easy that she can prepare dinner for her family in just 10 minutes.

INGREDIENTS:

- 1 pound extra-lean, grass-fed, Big Island ground beef
- 1 tablespoon chili powder
- 1 cup fat-free, reduced-sodium chicken broth
- 1 cup water
- 2 cups instant white rice, uncooked
- ½ cup Cheez Whiz cheese dip
- 2 cups lettuce, shredded
- 1 large Big Island tomato, chopped

PREPARATION:

Wash, trim and chop the tomato; wash, trim, and shred the lettuce. Set aside.

Brown the meat in a large frying pan. When it's browned, add the chili powder, broth and water, stir, and bring to boil. Stir in the rice and Cheez Whiz; cover. Simmer on low heat for 5 minutes, stirring constantly.

Serve topped with the lettuce and tomatoes.

Roast Turkey in a KTA Paper Sack
SERVES 12

Many Big Island families rely on this simple technique to roast their Thanksgiving turkeys to perfection. It's turkey magic, using something as simple as a KTA paper sack!

Try this turkey with the Wiki Wiki Fruit Chutney on page 123.

INGREDIENTS:

1 (12 to 15 pound) turkey, thawed
Brine (1 gallon water and ¼ cup coarse salt)
1 medium-size onion
1 (10 ounce) Portuguese sausage
1 cup (2 sticks) butter
Garlic salt, to taste
Black pepper, to taste
2 tablespoons canola oil
1 brown paper grocery bag, clean, large enough to hold the whole
turkey

PREPARATION:

Remove the turkey neck and the package of innards stuffed in the turkey cavity. Mix the brine in a large pot and submerge the turkey in the brine for at least eight hours in the refrigerator. I use a two gallon ziplock bag for brining.

When you're ready to stuff the turkey, preheat the oven to 350°F. Peel and coarsely chop the onion. Cut the Portuguese sausage into ¼-inch slices and then into chunks.

Remove the turkey from the brine and dry with paper towel. Place the chopped onion and sausage, and 1 stick of butter, inside the turkey cavity.

Melt the other stick of butter in a small pan or in the microwave, and baste the entire turkey with the butter. Sprinkle the turkey with the garlic salt and pepper and rub with your clean hands, evenly distributing the flavor over the whole bird.

(recipe continued on page 16)

Rub the canola oil into the bottom of the paper sack. The bottom should be saturated with oil. Do not oil the entire sack. Put the sack in a roasting pan and then place the turkey in the sack. Fold over the edges of the sack and staple shut.

Cook the turkey in a 350°F oven for 4 hours. Internal temperature should read 180°. Allow to rest for 10 minutes.

PRESENTATION:

Remove the turkey from the sack before serving. Remove the sausage and onion, then slice and serve on the side of the turkey. You can serve the bird whole and carve at the table, or you can remove and shred the turkey meat and serve it on a platter. If you don't want to make gravy with the juice from the bottom of the pan, just serve the juice in a gravy boat, or pour it over the shredded turkey on the platter.

This paper-sack turkey is guaranteed to be super moist and delicious!

Kim Chee Clam Dip
MAKES 1½ CUPS

Robin Kokubun, KTA Super Stores inventory clerk, likes to serve this dip with crudités and potato chips.

INGREDIENTS:
- 1 block cream cheese, softened
- ½ cup mayonnaise
- 1 tablespoon Worcestershire sauce
- 1 can (6 ounce) ajitsuke clams, partially drained
- ½ bottle kim chee, chopped coarsely
- 2 tablespoons kim chee juice

PREPARATION:

An hour or so before you're going to make the dip, set the cream cheese out to soften.

Mix together the softened cream cheese, mayonnaise, and Worcestershire sauce. Add the clams and some of their juice, then the kim chee and the kim chee juice. Mix well.

Serve with crudités or your favorite potato chips.

Apple Vinaigrette
MAKES 1½ CUPS

Lori Taniguchi is the daughter of Tony and Yasuko Taniguchi and lives on the mainland. This is one of her favorite salad dressings.

INGREDIENTS:
- 1 tablespoon Dijon mustard
- 6 tablespoons balsamic vinegar
- 1 tablespoon extra virgin olive oil
- 3 garlic cloves, peeled and finely minced
- ½ cup apple juice

PREPARATION:

Pour all ingredients into a jar, cover tightly, and shake well.

Kim Chee and Togan Soup
SERVES 8

Togan is a very large Asian squash, sometimes called winter melon or wax gourd. It's often made into soup, where its mild taste can be spiked with stronger flavors.

This version of togan soup is a winner. It is mild enough that even children will enjoy it, but flavorful enough that it will impress friends at potlucks and pūpū parties.

INGREDIENTS:

1 package (1¼ pound) ground pork
5 slices ginger (peeled and sliced ½-inch thick) OR 2 tablespoons prepared minced ginger
Approximately 40 (1½-inch) cubes of peeled and seeded togan
  (will require approximately one 4-pound togan squash)
1 bottle (12 ounce) regular Kohala brand Kim Chee, chopped fine, with
  juice OR, your favorite kim chee
1 (20 ounce) block firm tofu, cut into 2-inch cubes
5 (14.5 ounce) cans of chicken broth

PREPARATION:

If you're using fresh ginger, peel it (try scraping it with the blunt edge of a spoon) and slice it ½-inch thick. If you're pressed for time, you can use the prepared minced ginger that comes in a jar.

Peel and trim the togan squash, and cut it into 1½-inch cubes. Any extra can be frozen and used in other dishes, or for another pot of soup. Chop the kim chee and the tofu.

Heat a frying pan over medium-high heat and brown the ground pork and the ginger. When the pork is cooked, put a lid or a flat sieve over the pan and carefully drain off the excess fat.

Put the cooked pork, the chicken broth, fresh or frozen togan, and kim chee in a large soup pot. Simmer over medium heat for at least 30 minutes, or until the togan is tender but not falling apart. Add the tofu cubes and cook for a few more minutes, until the tofu is warm. Add salt to taste. You may not need much if you've used salted chicken broth.

Sesame Seed Chicken
SERVES 6

This roasted chicken dish is delightfully sweet and tart; it's also easy to prepare. The recipe comes from Jon Taniguchi, Tony and Yasuko Taniguchi's son.

INGREDIENTS:
2 whole roasting chickens (approximately 4½ pounds each)
1 cup Dijon mustard
1 cup apricot preserves
2 tablespoons sesame seeds (you can use either raw or toasted seeds)

PREPARATION:
Preheat the oven to 350°F.

Mix the mustard and preserves. Rub the spicy paste on the chickens, inside and out. Put the chickens, breast side up, into a roasting pan (or two, if you don't have one pan sufficiently large), and sprinkle the sesame seeds over the top of the chickens.

Bake uncovered in the pre-heated oven for about one hour. When an instant-read thermometer inserted in the meaty part of the thigh registers 155 to 165°F, the chickens are done.

PRESENTATION:
Serve with rice or mashed potatoes, and freshly-cooked vegetables.

1/4/2011: D/ me; added salt, pepper - put in deep dish cooker over grill - halved recipe over an hour to grill! too dry.

Best of the Big Island

Every year, three Big Island newspapers—the *Hawai'i Tribune Herald*, *West Hawai'i Today*, and *North Hawai'i News*—poll their readers. Who's the best on the Big Island? Best auto dealership? Best beach? Best museum? Best seafood restaurant? Best plate lunch?

I'm always on the lookout for outstanding recipes, so of course I had to visit some of the perennial food category winners and ask them to share some of their most popular recipes. Here are a few of my finds.

AKA Sushi's Spicy 'Ahi
MAKES 4 HANDROLLS

In 2009, newspaper readers agreed that the best sushi place in North Hawai'i was AKA Sushi. This small outfit is located in the Kamuela Deli, at the Waimea Shopping Center. It's run by Kyaw and Akiko Moe, who've been selling their tasty delicacies since 2007. Kyaw graciously shared his recipe for spicy 'ahi, a favorite filling for AKA's makizushi, or roll sushi. You can also serve this filling as if it were poke—it's good enough to stand by itself.

Be sure to use the red masago roe, not the green. The green roe is mixed with wasabi; you don't want that taste here.

INGREDIENTS:
- 1 pound sashimi-grade local-caught 'ahi (tuna), chopped fine; no pieces larger than ⅛-inch
- 1 tablespoon tobiko (flying fish roe) OR 1 tablespoon masago (capelin roe)
- ½ teaspoon Sriracha hot sauce; add more if you like it hot
- 2 tablespoons green onions, finely chopped
- 1 teaspoon sesame oil

PREPARATION:

Once you've assembled the ingredients and chopped the 'ahi and onion, you're almost done. Mix all the ingredients and use as filling for makizushi. If you don't know how to make makizushi, you can follow the directions for Sansei's Shrimp Tempura Hand Roll, page 171. Just substitute the spicy 'ahi for the shrimp tempura.

Lily's Sukiyaki
SERVES 8

Lily Inouye is one of the Big Island's most re-
spected seniors. She raised a happy, close-knit
family, helped out at her husband's business, and
devoted much time and effort to her church and
to local charities. She even found time to finish a
college degree that had been interrupted by World
War II.

Lily remembers growing up during the plantation
days of the 1920s and 1930s. At that time, many
housewives bought food from grocery trucks. The
trucks sold packaged foods, canned goods, and
fresh chicken, beef, and pork on ice. A vendor would drive into a plantation camp or resi-
dential neighborhood and ring a bell; housewives would come out to inspect the merchandise
and make their weekly purchases. Few working families had refrigerators or iceboxes in
those days, so meat and poultry from the truck were often cooked right away. Sukiyaki was
one way to savor the weekly treat.

Sukiyaki was a big event in Lily's household. Lily remembers her father heating up the
charcoal stove and getting ready to cook the sukiyaki while her mother was hard at work
in the kitchen, prepping all the ingredients. Lily's father was very proud of "his" tasty
sukiyaki, even though his wife had done most of the work.

Here's Lily's sukiyaki, just as her family prepared it in those long-ago plantation days.

If you're going to use beef, be sure to buy the best beef you can afford. Premium steak
cuts, such as strip (top loin), T-bone, Porterhouse, rib-eye, rib, and tenderloin will give
the best results.

INGREDIENTS:

- **2 pounds tender beef, thinly sliced OR 2 pounds boneless, skinless chicken, cut into bite-size pieces**
- **1½ pounds shirataki (yam cake noodles) OR 2 ounces long rice (also called bean thread or cellophane noodles)**
- **(long rice is often sold in 1-ounce bundles)**
- **1 block firm tofu, cut into 1-inch cubes**
- **1 large gobo (burdock root)**
- **1 large or 2 medium-size yellow or red onions, peeled and cut into ⅛-inch slices**
- **1 (11 ounce) can button mushrooms, drained OR ¼ pound fresh enoki mushrooms, roots removed**
- **1 (16 ounce) can of bamboo shoots, rinsed and cut into ¼-inch slices**

For the garnish:
1 bunch green onions, washed and cut into 3-inch pieces, OR 1 bunch watercress, washed and cut into 1-inch pieces

For the sauce:
½ cup soy sauce
⅓ cup sugar
¾ cup mirin
¼ cup water
¼ cup sake (Japanese rice wine)
1 (1.4 ounce) package dashi-no-moto (no MSG added)

PREPARATION:

Just like Lily's mother, you're going to have to put some time into prepping all the ingredients. You'll want to:

- Cut up the beef or chicken and store it, covered, in the refrigerator while you prepare the rest of the ingredients.

- If you are using shirataki noodles, rinse them well. If you are using long rice, soak it in warm water until soft, drain it, and cut it into 3-inch lengths.

- Cut up the tofu.

- Scrape the brown skin from the gobo with the back of a knife or the blunt edge of a spoon. Cut it into 2-inch long matchsticks.

- Prepare the rest of the sukiyaki vegetables as directed in the ingredients list.

- Mix the sukiyaki sauce.

Just before you are ready to eat, arrange the beef or chicken, the noodles, the tofu, and all the vegetable ingredients attractively on a serving platter or in serving bowls.

Sukiyaki is usually cooked at the table, as everyone watches hungrily. Put the prepped food and a sukiyaki pan (a heavy, thick, shallow pot available in Asian stores), on a hot plate near the cook's place at the table. (You can also use an electric frying pan.) Call the family and start cooking!

Heat up the pan and add just enough canola oil to coat it. Sauté the beef or chicken pieces until they are half-cooked. Add the tofu, shirataki if you are using it, the gobo, onions, mushrooms, and bamboo shoots. (If you have decided to use long rice, wait and add it later.) Season with sukiyaki sauce to taste. Cover the pan, turn the heat to high, and bring the sukiyaki to a boil. Do not let it boil for

(recipe continued on page 26)

more than a minute or two; reduce the heat and simmer for another 4 minutes. Be sure to stir occasionally, so that the sauce is evenly distributed and everything is well-cooked.

After you've simmered the sukiyaki, add the long rice, if you are using long rice instead of shirataki. Note that long rice, even pre-soaked long rice, will absorb a lot of liquid. You may need to add a little extra sauce.

Sprinkle the chopped green onions or watercress over the top of the sukiyaki, cover the pan again, and simmer for 2 more minutes.

PRESENTATION:

Let each person ladle his or her serving into his or her own bowl. If you need to cook extra servings, you can push the cooked ingredients to one side of the pan and add more of the raw ingredients. You may need to mix up and add extra sauce. Don't just add water and dilute the sauce.

Shoyu Poke, KTA-Style
MAKES 4 CUPS

Best poke place in East Hawai'i? According to the Hawai'i Tribune Herald *poll, it's KTA Super Stores.*

Here's a KTA recipe that makes enough shoyu poke for a lū'au. If you're making it for a small family, be sure to cut down the recipe.

You can make this with 'ahi, marlin, cooked octopus, imitation crab meat, mussels, or just about any seafood that's fresh and local.

INGREDIENTS:
- 5 pounds fresh seafood
- 2 cups thinly-sliced or minced sweet local onions (about ½ pound of onions)
- 2 cups ogo (about one (4 ounce) bag), cleaned and chopped into 2-inch pieces
- ½ cup chopped green onions (about 4 stalks)
- 2 tablespoons sesame oil
- 2 tablespoons toasted sesame seeds
- 1 cup Mountain Apple Brand poke or seafood marinade (available at KTA Super Stores, in the seafood department)

PREPARATION:

Cut fish into ¾-inch cubes, octopus and mussel into thin strips, imitation crab meat into 1-inch pieces. Whatever seafood you use, you want it in bite-size pieces.

Put the different kids of seafood into separate containers; do not mix them.

Chop the onions and ogo per the instuctions in the ingredients list and sprinkle them over the seafood.

Shake the bottle of seafood marinade, so that it's well-mixed, and pour 1 cup of marinade into a mixing bowl. Add the sesame seeds and sesame oil and mix well.

Pour the marinade over the seafood. Gently mix the poke so that the onions and ogo are well-mixed and everything is coated with marinade. Serve immediately.

Creamy Seafood Pesto Over Linguine
SERVES 6

Don's Grill has been winning the Best Family Restaurant award for East Hawai'i for many years. I've always found them family-friendly and reasonably priced, and enjoyed the great food they serve.

Here's the recipe for one of their delicious pastas, as prepared by proprietor Don Hoota.

INGREDIENTS:
12 large shrimp, peeled and deveined
½ pound mahimahi fillet, cut into ¾ inch cubes
½ pound scallops, cut in half, horizontally
1 pound linguine
1 tablespoon canola or coconut oil, for sautéing the seafood
2 tablespoons grated Parmesan cheese, as garnish (note that you'll also need grated cheese for the sauce)

For the pesto sauce:
4 cups fresh basil leaves, de-stemmed, lightly packed
⅓ cup olive oil
3 cloves garlic, chopped
¼ cup macadamia nuts
½ cup grated Parmesan or Romano cheese
¾ cup whipping cream
Salt and white pepper to taste

PREPARATION:
Prepare the seafood as directed in the ingredient list and set aside.

Set a large pot of water to boil and add the linguine. Cook for 9 to 10 minutes, or until the pasta is al dente (cooked, but still a little firm). Drain and rinse the pasta.

Put the basil leaves, olive oil, garlic, macadamia nuts, and grated cheese in a food processor and purée. If you don't have a food processor, you can use a blender, though you might have to add a little water.

Scrape the basil purée into a bowl and add the cream. Mix well. Add salt and pepper to taste. Set aside.

Place a large frying pan over medium-high heat and add 1 tablespoon oil. When the oil is hot, add the cut-up seafood and sauté for a scant 2 to 3 minutes. Do not over-cook the seafood, or it will be tough.

(recipe continued on page 30)

Remove from the heat and add to the pesto sauce.

To serve family style, mound the linguine on a platter and pour the seafood and pesto over the pasta. Top with an additional sprinkling of shredded Parmesan cheese.

Kona Coffee Crisp Tulips with Two Kona Coffee Liqueur Mousses
MAKES 20 TULIP CUPS

Kailua Candy Company was voted the best place to buy candy and cookies in West Hawai'i. This Kailua-Kona retail store is run by proprietors Cathy Smoot Barrett and husband Robin Barrett, chocolatiers par excellence.

Their two-mousse tulip cups require a fair bit of time and effort, but you won't need to buy any special equipment to make them. Cathy and Robin use small balloons as a foundation for edible chocolate cups, and whip up two kinds of chocolate mousse to fill the cups. The filled cups look gorgeous and taste great. Try this one when you have some extra time and want to impress your family or some special guests.

INGREDIENTS:

For the tulips:
20 small balloons
1 pound best-quality Hawaiian dark chocolate
1 cup coarsely chopped, dry-roasted Big Island macadamia nuts
1 cup coarsely chopped 100% Kona coffee beans, dark roast

For the dark chocolate mousse:
½ pound best-quality Hawaiian dark chocolate
⅓ cup best-quality Kona coffee liqueur
1 egg white
½ cup heavy cream

For the white chocolate Kona coffee liqueur mousse:
½ pound best-quality white chocolate
⅓ cup best-quality Kona coffee liqueur
1 egg white
½ cup heavy cream
(All in all, you'll need ⅔ cup liqueur, 2 large eggs, and 1 cup of heavy cream.)

PREPARATION:

To prepare the tulip cups: Blow up all the balloons so that they are all about 3 inches in diameter. Carefully melt the dark chocolate in a double boiler over a pan of hot water, kept at 100°F.

Do not let even a drop of water touch the chocolate; it will seize! That means that it will become dull and grainy. Once it has seized, you can't restore it to its initial smoothness.

Mix the ground Kona coffee and macadamia nuts into the melted chocolate.

Dip the blown up water balloons carefully into the melted chocolate mixture. Dip to one side, and then another to form petals, like a tulip.

Set the chocolate-covered balloons on a large baking pan lined with parchment paper. Allow to cool and set hard. You can speed this up a little if you put the pan in the refrigerator for 1 hour.

When the cups are set hard, pop the balloons and carefully peel them out of the chocolate tulip. Store the tulip cups in a cool, dry place.

To prepare the mousses: Melt the white and dark chocolate separately, using a double boiler with the top set over but not in simmering water.

Measure out the Kona coffee liqueur and whisk ⅓ cup into each pan of chocolate.

Separate the eggs, taking care that not a speck of yolk is mixed with the whites. Whip the egg whites until stiff. Fold half of the egg whites into each pan of chocolate.

Whip the heavy cream until it holds a soft peak and carefully fold half of the cream into each pan of mousse.

Scoop a little dark chocolate mousse and white chocolate mousse into each chocolate tulip cup.

You can store the tulip cups, covered, in the refrigerator if you aren't planning on serving them immediately. Don't let the cups get wet; they will look blotchy and ugly.

Spaghetti Squash with Pesto
SERVES 4

Island Naturals Market and Deli recently moved into larger quarters at the Hilo Shopping Center. That's testimony to owner Russell Ruderman's hard work and fine food. Further proof came in 2009, when the deli was voted best place in East Hawai'i for vegetarian food.

One of the signature dishes at Island Naturals is this extremely easy spaghetti squash with pesto. You might want to make a double batch of the delicious pesto, which can be used in many other dishes.

INGREDIENTS:
1 medium size spaghetti squash
Olive oil

For the pesto:
¼ pound sweet basil or a mixture of
  basil and mint leaves
2 to 3 tablespoons olive oil
1 medium-size clove garlic, peeled
¼ cup roasted pine nuts
Salt and pepper to taste
Parmesan cheese (optional)

PREPARATION:
Put the basil leaves, pine nuts, garlic, salt and pepper into a food processor or blender. Turn on the machine, then drizzle the olive oil into the other ingredients, little by little, until you have a smooth sauce.

Preheat the oven to 350°F. Cut the squash in half, lengthwise, and remove the seeds. Rub olive oil all over the squash and put it in a baking dish. Bake the squash for 45 minutes to 1 hour, or until soft.

PRESENTATION:
Use an ice cream scoop to scoop the squash pulp out of the skin. Put several balls of squash on each serving plate. Pour some pesto sauce over each ball of squash.

If you have leftover squash, just seal it into plastic bags or containers and freeze, to thaw and reheat later. Leftover pesto can be put in the refrigerator, where it will keep for several months.

Furikake Salmon
SERVES 4

Hilo's Seaside Restaurant is a perennial winner of the Best Place for Seafood award in the Hawai'i Tribune Herald's annual poll. Furikake salmon is always on the menu and is one of the restaurant's most popular dishes.

This recipe calls for wasabi powder. You can also use the wasabi paste that comes in tubes. Note that many of the powders and pastes that you can buy in the supermarket are actually made from horseradish, rather than real wasabi root—which is hard to cultivate and fairly expensive. It is up to you whether you use horseradish wasabi or real wasabi.

You'll end up with more teriyaki sauce than you need for this dish. Most Island households will use up the extra sauce in no time!

INGREDIENTS:
2 (8 to 9 ounce) salmon fillets (1 pound or slightly more, in total)
1 cup furikake
2 tablespoons canola oil

For the teriyaki sauce:
2 cups soy sauce
2 cups sugar
2 tablespoons garlic, minced
2 tablespoons ginger, minced
2 tablespoons mirin
2 tablespoons cornstarch
¼ cup cold water

For the wasabi mayonnaise:
1 cup mayonnaise
2 tablespoons wasabi powder
2 tablespoons water

PREPARATION:

To prepare the teriyaki sauce: Put the soy sauce, sugar, garlic, ginger, and mirin in a small pot and bring to a boil. Lower the heat.

Prepare a cornstarch slurry by thoroughly mixing the cornstarch and the cold water. No lumps, or you'll have lumps in your sauce!

Add the slurry, whisk, and keep on simmering and whisking the sauce as it thickens. It should be about the thickness of maple syrup when done. Remove from heat and set aside.

(recipe continued on page 34)

To prepare the wasabi mayonnaise: Mix the wasabi powder and the water until you have a smooth paste. Mix the wasabi paste with the mayonnaise.

To cook the fish: Preheat your oven to 350°F and line a small pan or baking sheet with parchment.

Spread the furikake over the bottom of a shallow pan or on a plate, and dredge the salmon fillets in the furikake until they are completely coated.

Heat a medium-size frying pan over high heat. Add 2 tablespoons canola oil and sear the salmon fillets on both sides.

Transfer the seared salmon to the parchment-lined dish and bake in the pre-heated oven for 10 to 15 minutes, or until the fish is cooked through.

PRESENTATION:

Pour ¼ cup of the teriyaki sauce into the middle of a serving platter. Place the furikake salmon fillets on top of the teriyaki sauce and drizzle wasabi mayonnaise around the salmon.

Walnut Rice Cereal Bars
MAKES 28 (2 x 2 INCH) BARS

Readers of the North Hawai'i News *picked Waimea's Leilani Bakery as the best bakery in North Hawai'i. Proprietors Kevin and Leilani Kusano kindly shared this very easy recipe for walnut rice cereal bars. Once you've shopped for the ingredients, you've done most of the work!*

INGREDIENTS:

3¼ cups walnut halves and pieces
1½ cups dried cranberries (one 6 ounce package yields 1½ cups)
1½ cups puffed rice cereal
½ stick unsalted butter, melted
2 (10.5 ounce) bags large marshmallows

For the topping:
1 bag semi-sweet chocolate morsels
½ cup walnuts, finely chopped

PREPARATION:

Spray a 9 x 13 inch baking sheet pan with non-stick spray.

Add the walnuts, cranberries, and rice cereal to a large bowl and mix well. Melt the butter over low heat. Add the marshmallows to the melted butter and stir continuously until the marshmallows have melted.

Pour the melted marshmallow/butter mixture over the rice cereal mixture. Stir and toss with a spatula until well combined. Once the mixture cools a little, you can coat your (washed and clean) hands with nonstick spray and mix with your hands. The mixture will be sticky and stiff.

Press the mixture firmly into the baking pan. The surface should be flat and even. Cool to room temperature.

To prepare the topping: Melt chocolate morsels until smooth and spread over the surface of the bars. Sprinkle evenly with walnuts, pressing them into the chocolate.

Cut the bars into squares and serve.

Risotto alla Milanese
with Seared Sea Scallops
SERVES 2 TO 3

Readers of the North Hawai'i News chose Solimene's at the Waimea Center as the best Italian restaurant in North Hawai'i. It's owned and operated by the Aiona family. One of their most popular dishes is this risotto with scallops.

If you can't find Grana Padano cheese, you can substitute a good Parmesan or Romano.

This is not dish that you can simmer on the stove and check from time to time. You will be stirring the risotto constantly; if you don't, it will be lumpy rather than deliciously creamy. Make this on a day when you have time to cook. You will find the results well worth it!

INGREDIENTS:
- 4 + 2 tablespoons olive oil
- 2 + 1 tablespoon unsalted butter
- 1 medium-size yellow onion, cut into ½-inch dice
- 1 cup Italian super-fine Arborio rice
- ¾ teaspoon saffron threads
- ⅓ cup white wine (Solimeme's likes a pinot grigio)
- 4 to 5 cups chicken stock or broth
- ½ cup grated Grana Padano cheese (cheese may be omitted if you prefer not to serve cheese with seafood, serving them together is the custom in Italy)
- Freshly ground black pepper
- 8 sea scallops, patted dry, salted and peppered

PREPARATION:
Prepare the onion, grated cheese, and scallops per the directions in the ingredients list. Assemble all ingredients.

Set a heavy pan or Dutch oven over medium heat; add 2 tablespoons butter and 4 tablespoons olive oil. When the butter has melted, add the diced onions and sweat until soft and opaque, but not browned. Add the rice and continue to cook the onions and rice, stirring frequently, until the rice is opaque rather than translucent. This should take about 10 minutes.

Sprinkle the saffron threads over the rice and stir to combine. Add white wine and continue to stir and cook on medium heat until the rice has absorbed all the wine. Heat the chicken broth, either in the microwave or on the stove. Reduce the heat under the rice to medium-low and ladle ½ cup of the hot broth over the rice. It should just cover the rice. Stir constantly until all the stock is absorbed. Repeat this process until the rice is tender and most of the stock is gone; this should take about 17 to 20 minutes.

As noted above, it is very important to keep stirring throughout this process, so that your rice comes out tender and creamy, not lumpy.

When the last of the stock is almost totally absorbed, add 1 tablespoon of cold butter and the grated cheese (if you're using cheese). Stir vigorously. Remove the risotto pan from the heat, cover it, and let it sit while you prepare the scallops.

Place a frying pan over high heat and add 2 tablespoons of olive oil. When the oil is hot, add the scallops. Sear each side until just golden brown, 2 to 4 minutes on each side.

PRESENTATION:

You can serve this on individual serving plates, or family-style on a platter. Mound risotto on the plate or platter and spoon sautéed scallops over the top. Sprinkle with freshly-ground pepper and serve immediately.

Korean-Style Squid
MAKES 2 CUPS

GW Construction won for best contractor, but the owners, Gerald and Wendy, also make a mean marinated squid. I just had to include it here. After you taste it, I think you'll agree that they also deserve to win the Best of Squid award … that is, if there were such a thing.

Wendy Yamada learned how to make this dish from her dad, Gerald Nagata. Thank you for sharing, Wendy!

INGREDIENTS:
- 3 pounds whole squid
- 2 cups boiling water
- 1 teaspoon garlic salt

For the sauce:
- ¾ cup soy sauce
- 3 tablespoon lemon juice
- 4 stalks green onion, chopped
- 1 Maui onion, sliced thinly, ⅛-inch
- 1 Hawaiian chili pepper, chopped fine
- 2 tablespoons sesame seeds, toasted
- ¼ cup sesame oil

PREPARATION:

Clean the squid, if it isn't already cleaned (See step-by-step instructions on page 128-129). Slice squid into 1½ inch strips and score lightly. Bring 2 cups water to boil. Add 1 teaspoons garlic salt. Stir squid in boiling water for 1 minute (don't overcook).

Drain and cool. Mix remaining ingredients together. Marinate squid in sauce overnight.

Agricultural Industries

The Big Island is the agricultural powerhouse of the Hawaiian island chain. It has 680,000 acres under cultivation—that's 62 percent of the farmland in the state. Big Island farmers are growing over 40 different crops ... and may be growing even more in the future, as they experiment with new crops and find cultivars that grow well in our climate and soils.

Here are just a few recipes that feature some of the Big Island's signature agricultural products. Eating local foods is the newest food trend, as savvy consumers reduce their carbon footprint and enjoy the freshest, juiciest produce. Hop on the bandwagon!

Chip and Macadamia Nut Cookie Cups
MAKES 5 DOZEN COOKIE CUPS

Sixty percent of the state's macadamia nuts are grown and processed on the Big Island. The industry brings $38.9 million a year into our Island economy.

The first macadamia nut trees were planted in Kea'au in 1946. The area has remained at the center of the macadamia industry, thanks to Kea'au's Mauna Loa Macadamia Nut Factory (the largest in the world; now owned by Hershey, once owned by Castle and Cook).

Island cooks have been experimenting with macadamia nuts for decades. We eat macadamia-crusted fish and chicken, sprinkle the nuts on pies and ice cream, and make all sorts of nutty candies and baked goods. Here's a sinfully rich recipe for mini-tarts with cream cheese, chocolate, coconut, sweetened condensed milk, and macadamia nuts. The recipe can also be found on the Mauna Loa Macadamia website.

You'll need at least one 24-cup mini-tart pan to bake these cookie cups. It would be ideal to bake them all at once, in three pans. If you don't have three pans, you'll have to bake in successive batches.

INGREDIENTS:
1 cup (2 sticks) butter, softened
1 (8 ounce) package cream cheese, less 2 ounces, softened
2 cups white all-purpose flour
½ cup sugar
1 cup Hershey's Special Dark chocolate chips
1 cup Mounds sweetened coconut flakes
½ cup Mauna Loa Macadamia nut baking pieces
2 eggs
1 (14 ounce) can sweetened condensed milk (not evaporated milk)
2 tablespoons light corn syrup
1 teaspoon Hawaiian vanilla extract
½ teaspoon coconut extract
⅛ teaspoon salt

PREPARATION:
Cream the butter and cream cheese together in a large bowl. Gradually add the flour and sugar, beating until well-blended. If the dough is too soft to shape easily, cover and refrigerate the dough until it has stiffened a little.

Divide the dough into 5 equal parts. Roll each of the lumps of dough into a long "noodle," then cut each noodle into 12 equal pieces. Roll the pieces into smooth balls. Shape each part into 12 smooth balls. Place each ball in a mini-muffin cup (each cup should be 1¾ inches in diameter. Press the dough down on the bottom and up onto the sides, forming a tiny tart cup.

AGRICULTURAL INDUSTRIES

Pre-heat your oven to 375°F. While it is heating, mix the chocolate chips, coconut flakes, and macadamia nut pieces together; spoon the mixture into the tart cups. Do your best to evenly divide the mixture into three batches.

Beat the eggs in small bowl. Add the sweetened condensed milk, corn syrup, vanilla extract, coconut extract, and salt. Mix well. Spoon the egg-and-milk mixture into the cups, dividing as equally as you can.

Bake the filled tin or tins for 18 to 20 minutes, or until the tops are puffed and turn light golden brown. Cool completely in pan; set the pans on a wire rack for more even cooling. Remove the cookie cups from the pan or pans using a small metal spatula or a sharp knife. Store tightly covered at room temperature.

Alan Wong's
Hāmākua Springs Stewed Tomatoes
MAKES 2 CUPS

Celebrity chef Alan Wong buys as many of his ingredients as he can right here in the Islands. He has always been a big supporter of Big Island farmers, ranchers, and fishermen.

Chef Alan kindly shared this shared this yummy stewed tomato recipe, which is best made with tomatoes from Richard Ha's Hāmākua Springs Country Farm. If you've never tasted truly fresh stewed tomatoes, you're in for a treat.

INGREDIENTS:

2 medium-size red Hāmākua Springs tomatoes, cut into large ½-inch dice
1 teaspoon chili pepper water (see next recipe)
1 + 1 teaspoons minced garlic
12 red Hāmākua Springs cocktail tomatoes
2 tablespoons tomato paste
8 basil leaves, torn
¼ teaspoon sugar
1 teaspoon apple cider vinegar
¼ cup extra virgin olive oil
Salt, to taste

PREPARATION:

Trim and dice the large tomatoes. Put the diced tomatoes, chili pepper water, and one teaspoon of the minced garlic in a blender. Purée until smooth. Pour the mixture into a medium size saucepan and reserve until ready to use.

TO PEEL THE COCKTAIL TOMATOES:

- Cut a small "x" on the tip of the tomato (opposite the stem). Use a small knife and cut very lightly; you want to lightly pierce the skin, not cut into the flesh of the tomato.

- Prepare a bowl of ice water and set some water to boil in a medium-size sauce pot. Blanch the tomatoes in the boiling water for 10 to 15 seconds. Immediately remove the tomatoes from the boiling water and submerge them in the ice water.

- When the tomatoes are cool, peel off the skin. The skin near the "x-cut" will have pulled away from the flesh slightly; you can start peeling there. Discard the skin, and add the peeled tomatoes to the pureed mixture in the saucepan.

Add the tomato paste to the sauce pan. Mix carefully to avoid breaking the peeled tomatoes. Simmer on medium heat for 10 minutes. Next, add the remaining 1 teaspoon of garlic, and the sugar, vinegar, and olive oil. Stir gently to combine the ingredients and season with salt to taste. Turn off the heat, and reserve until ready to use.

You can cover and store the stewed tomatoes in the refrigerator; they will keep for several weeks.

Alan Wong's Chili Pepper Water
MAKES 1½ CUPS

INGREDIENTS:

   ⅓ plus 1¼ cups cold water
   ½ clove garlic
   2 red Hawaiian chilies OR 1 red Serrano pepper,
      OR 1 red jalapeño pepper
   2 tablespoons white vinegar
   2 teaspoons minced ginger
   1 teaspoon salt, or to taste

PREPARATION:
Trim, halve, and seed the pepper or peppers.

Put the ⅓ cup water, garlic, chilies, vinegar, ginger, and salt in a blender and purée until smooth.

Put the 1¼ cups of water in a saucepan and bring to a boil. Add the chili purée and return to a boil. As soon as the mixture has boiled, remove it from the heat and let it cool. When cool, transfer to an airtight container. Keep refrigerated.

Kawamata Farms Tomato Gazpacho
SERVES 4

Big Island farmer Naoji Kawamata grew roses in Lalamilo for many years. One year, he applied a new fungicide from a large, trusted company; his trust was misplaced. The fungicide killed his roses and contaminated his soil. His son Raymond rescued the family farm by starting a hydroponic tomato farm, based on a system perfected in the Netherlands. The tomatoes never touch the ground, but grow in a nutrient solution that produces some of the biggest, juiciest tomatoes you've ever tasted.

Chef Piet Wigmans, executive chef for the Hilo Hawaiian Hotel, was given a crate of the luscious Kawamata tomatoes and showcased them in the following gazpacho (cold tomato soup).

Chef Piet fire-roasts the tomatoes over the gas grill in his restaurant. To fire-roast, cut the tomatoes in half, lengthwise, and brush some olive oil on the cut surfaces. Put them on the grill, over a medium-hot flame, and let them cook until they develop dark char marks. This may take about 5 to 8 minutes. Turn the tomatoes over with tongs; cook the other side. Remove and cool. Once the tomatoes have cooled, you can peel off the skin.

If you don't have a gas or charcoal grill, or don't want to bother with fire-roasting, you can simply blanch and peel the tomatoes, as described in the recipe. The soup will still be tasty; it will just lack the hint of "campfire cooking" you get from the fire-roasted tomatoes.

INGREDIENTS:
6 ripe Kawamata tomatoes
1 cup vegetable stock
½ medium-size red onion, diced
1 cup Hāmākua English cucumber, peeled, seeded, diced (⅛-inch dice)
½ teaspoon garlic, finely chopped (no pieces larger than ⅛-inch)
1 tablespoon fresh basil leaves, cut chiffonade, ⅛-inch wide
1 tablespoon Italian parsley, finely chopped
¼ cup extra virgin olive oil
2 tablespoons apple cider vinegar
1 teaspoon freshly ground black pepper
1 teaspoon salt
1 teaspoon chili pepper water (see recipe on page 43)

PREPARATION:

To blanch and peel the tomatoes (if you're not fire-roasting them):

Bring a pot of water to boil; prepare a large bowl of ice-water.

Lightly cut an X in the tomato skins, on the end opposite the stem. Blanch them in the boiling water until the cut skin starts to peel back, which should take about 1 minute. Immediately remove them from the boiling water and submerge them in the ice-water. After a minute or two, drain them and peel off the skin. Cut them in half and remove the seeds.

Instead of throwing away the seeds and the soft inner pulp, save them and put them in a blender. Add 1 cup of vegetable stock and blend. Strain the juice to remove any lingering seeds.

Chop the peeled tomatoes into ⅛-inch dice. Dice the onion; peel, seed, and dice the cucumber. All dice should be ⅛-inch. Peel and chop the garlic; no pieces should be larger than ⅛-inch. Stack the basil leaves and form them into a roll. Slice across the roll, cutting ⅛-inch-wide slivers. This is the chiffonade cut.

Put all the diced and cut vegetables into a large bowl or pot. Add the olive oil, vinegar, salt, pepper, and chili pepper water; cover and let sit for at least 4 hours, to allow the flavors to blend.

PRESENTATION:
Serve with garlic croutons or a slice of crusty bread.

Lemon-Mint Chicken Cutlets with Watercress
SERVES 4

Roy and Marlene Berger grow gourmet watercress on their 10-acre Mountain View farm. Berger's Kama'āina Farm produces the only land-grown watercress in the state. They are also the only watercress farm to have been certified by the state Food Safety Certification program. You can find their salad cress under the Mountain Apple Brand at KTA Stores, as well as at Whole Foods, Island Naturals, Times, and Foodland.

Watercress is sometimes bitter, but only if it is picked when it is too old, or hasn't been watered enough. I have always found the Berger watercress sweet and delicious. Fresh watercress is also highly nutritious. It's a good source of vitamin B6, vitamin C, manganese, carotenes, iron, calcium, and fiber. Your healthy, home-cooked food will be even healthier with a bit of cress.

I like to serve Berger cress with these lemon-mint cutlets.

INGREDIENTS:
- 1¼ pounds sliced skinless, boneless chicken breasts
- 2 medium-size lemons, sufficient for:
- 1 tablespoon + 1½ teaspoon grated lemon peel
- 3 tablespoons lemon juice
- 2 tablespoons olive oil
- 1 + 1 tablespoon chopped fresh mint
- 1 (4 ounce) bag Berger's Gourmet watercress, cut into 1-inch, bite-size pieces
- ½ teaspoon salt
- ½ teaspoon coarsely ground black pepper

PREPARATION:

Wash the chicken breasts and cut them into thin slices. Pound the slices with a meat mallet until they are uniformly ¼-inch thick.

Wash the lemons and grate the peel with a zester or microplane. If you've ended up with long strands of peel, chop them coarsely. Cut the lemons in half and squeeze them for juice. Measure out the 1 tablespoon + 1½ teaspoon of peel and the 3 tablespoons of juice for the dressing.

Wash and chop the mint and watercress. Set aside.

(recipe continued on page 48)

AGRICULTURAL INDUSTRIES

Whisk together the lemon peel and juice, olive oil, 1 tablespoon of the mint, salt, and pepper. Measure out and reserve ¼ cup of this dressing. Add the chicken cutlets to the remaining dressing and mix until the cutlets are thoroughly coated.

Heat a ridged grill pan over medium-high heat OR heat your outdoor grill to a medium-high heat).

Place the chicken in the grill pan or on the grill. Cook for 4 to 5 minutes or until the meat juices run clear when breast is pierced with the tip of a knife. Turn the cutlets at least once during cooking, so that both sides are grilled.

PRESENTATION:

Toss the watercress with the ¼ cup of reserved dressing and spread it on a serving platter. Arrange the chicken cutlets on the watercress. Sprinkle with the remaining tablespoon of chopped mint.

Baked Stuffed Avocado
SERVES 2

On the Big Island, we can buy fresh, local-grown avocados year-round. We see different varieties in the store at different times of year. My mother used to call them summer and winter avocados. Later I learned that we actually grow nine main varieties of avocado (Sharwil, Green Gold, Kahalu'u, Linda, Yamagata, Fujikawa, Murashige, Malama, Ota), many of which ripen at different times of the year. Not all summer avocados are the same.

Here is Hilo resident George Curtis's favorite way to prepare avocado. He notes that this recipe is highly flexible. If you've got a lot of avocado pulp, you may want to increase the poultry or chicken. You might want to add some extra seasonings. A bit of chopped basil gives extra zing.

Note that the recipe calls for ½ cup of cooked chicken, turkey, or shrimp. Many cooks will have a packet or container of leftovers in the freezer, ready for recipes just like this. If you don't have any pre-cooked poultry, you can buy what you need at a KTA deli counter. You'll find pre-cooked shrimp in the freezer section.

INGREDIENTS:
- 1 large, firm avocado
- ½ cup cooked, chopped chicken, turkey, or shrimp
- 1 tablespoon mayonnaise or Miracle Whip
- 1 teaspoon bacon bits
- ½ teaspoon seasoned salt
- ¼ teaspoon fresh, finely-ground black pepper

PREPARATION:
Preheat the oven to 350°F.

Select an avocado that is reasonably firm inside. Split it, remove the stem and seed, and scoop out some of the meat, leaving about ⅜-inch of meat in the shell. Cut the scooped-out meat into ½-inch dice. (A good size avocado should yield about ¾ cup of chopped avocado meat.)

Mix the chopped avocado, poultry or shrimp, mayonnaise or Miracle Whip, and bacon bits.

Dust the inside of the avocado halves with salt and pepper and pack the avocado mixture into the avocado shells. Arrange the halves in a baking pan and bake in the preheated oven for 20 minutes.

Preparing and Canning Fresh Bamboo Shoots
SERVES 6

I grew up eating fresh bamboo shoots cooked with pork, shoyu, and sugar. This traditional Asian dish was real comfort food. My family liked to give it an American touch: we ate it with mayonnaise!

We used to harvest our own bamboo shoots from large clusters of edible bamboo.

Nowadays most people buy their bamboo shoots at the local farmers' markets. The fresh shoots are only available during the spring and summer. If you want to eat them year-round, you have to cook and can them in season. It's a fair bit of work, but I think you'll find that the home-made shoots are ever so much better than the commercial canned variety.

INGREDIENTS:
Fresh bamboo shoots

PREPARATION:

Prepare the shoots immediately after you buy or gather them. If you let them sit, they get hard and bitter, and very quickly too.

Remove the outer green covering. The shoots should be perfectly white. Trim and discard all the tough and woody parts of the shoots. Test the shoots with a sharp knife; if they're difficult to cut, they're too tough. Cut the shoots into 2-inch long pieces. Split them if they are thicker than 1 inch. Cover with water and soak overnight. Change the water often during the afternoon and evening, and just before you go to bed at night.

The next morning, drain the shoots, add new water, and boil the shoots for 20 minutes. Drain the cooking water, add fresh water, and boil for another 20 minutes.

The shoots are now ready to eat. You can make the tasty pork dish that follows, or you can prepare traditional spring delicacies like takenoko gohan (bamboo-shoot rice).

TO CAN THE SHOOTS:

You'll need home canning equipment (large pot, jar rack, tongs, jars, lids, and screw bands) and some experience with canning if you're to produce completely safe products. If this is your first time canning, get a detailed guide or have an experienced canner show you the ropes.

Put the jar rack in the canning pot and fill it with clean, freshly-washed jars. Cover with water and bring to a boil. Turn the heat down slightly and keep the jars at a simmer.

Put the flat lids in a saucepan and cover with water; bring just to a simmer over medium heat. Do not boil. Reduce heat and keep them hot until you're ready to use them.

Put the screw bands near your work area. There's no need to heat the bands.

Use the tongs to pull a jar out of the hot water; fill the jar with bamboo shoots; completely cover them with bamboo cooking water. Leave a little space (head-space) between the liquid and the rim of the jar. Use the tongs to lift a lid out of the hot water and place it carefully on the rim of the jar. Screw the band around the jar and the lid. Tight, but not TOO tight. (This is where it helps to have an experienced canner on call.) Repeat until you've canned all the bamboo shoots. Put the jars back in the jar rack, make sure that they're covered with water, and bring the water to a boil. Boil the jars for ten minutes.

Congratulations! You can now eat home-canned bamboo shoots for the rest of the year.

Bamboo Shoots with Pork
SERVES 2

INGREDIENTS:
- ½ pound lean pork
- 2 cups sliced fresh bamboo shoots, prepared per directions on page 50
- 1 tablespoon canola oil
- ¼ cup soy sauce
- ⅓ cup brown sugar

PREPARATION:

Cut the pork into strips ¼-inch thick and 1-inch long. Cut the bamboo shoots into strips ⅛-inch thick and 1-inch long.

Heat the oil in a large pan or Dutch oven over medium heat; add the sliced pork and sauté for 2 to 3 minutes. Add the bamboo shoots and cook, stirring frequently, for another 10 minutes. Add the soy sauce and brown sugar, cover the pan, and simmer for 20 minutes. Serve over freshly-cooked rice.

Breadfruit or 'Ulu, Portuguese-Style
SERVES 6

'Ulu came to Hawai'i with the Native Hawaiians, so you could truthfully say that it's been an Island favorite for thousands of years. Many locals, of all ethnicities, have learned to love 'ulu; large breadfruit trees can be found in the back yards of many kama'āina homes.

Here's a Portuguese take on the crop: boil 'ulu slices in a vinho d'alhos marinade, then fry them in butter. I was given this local recipe by the Jarneski family of Hilo.

INGREDIENTS:
1 medium-size 'ulu
One head garlic, about 10 cloves
15 Hawaiian chili peppers (or fewer, if you don't like HOT)
2 tablespoons white distilled vinegar
¼ to ½ cup salt (add to taste)
Butter as needed for sautéing

PREPARATION:
Peel, quarter and core the breadfruit; peel and smash the garlic; trim and halve the chili peppers and remove the seeds. The garlic is smashed (you can do it with the flat of your knife blade) so that the clove is opened up, but is still in one loosely-connected piece.

Put the 'ulu in a large pot and add water to cover. Add the garlic, chilies, and vinegar. Add the salt a little at a time, tasting after each addition. Stop when it's just right.

Bring the water to a boil and then turn down the heat, simmering the 'ulu until it is fork-tender. This should take about 15 minutes. Do not overcook the breadfruit, or it will be too soft.

Remove the 'ulu from the pot, drain it, and cut it into 1-inch slices. Remove the smashed garlic cloves from the cooking liquid and smear them on top of the 'ulu slices.

Heat some butter in a frying pan and sauté the slices until they are nicely browned. Salt to taste and serve immediately.

Corn Salad
SERVES 8

Loeffler Farms is one of the Big Island's largest suppliers of sweet and delicious corn. They have 137 acres under cultivation in Kurtistown; they plant one acre every four days, so that there is an acre of corn ripening every four days or so. They can sell fresh Big Island corn year-round.

If you live Hilo-side, you can usually find the Loeffler corn stand in the parking lot of Kai Store, on the corner of Kīlauea and Puainako Street. The stand sells bags of one dozen ears, picked fresh that day. You'll want to cook it that day too; the corn loses its fresh, sweet flavor very rapidly.

It is so good that it tastes wonderful with minimal cooking. You can pop an ear in the microwave for 2 minutes, peel away the husks, and enjoy. Fresh corn is also wonderful when grilled. Soak the ears, still in their husks, in cold water for 10 minutes. Heat up the grill and grill the ears for another 10 minutes or so, turning once or twice so that they're evenly cooked. Whether you like your corn microwaved or grilled, with shoyu or with butter, this corn is delicious!

I also like to use fresh Loeffler corn in this colorful, crunchy, healthy salad.

The recipe calls for 6 ears of corn; average ears will yield about 3½ cups of fresh corn.

There are two schools of thought re cutting corn kernels off the cob. Some people like to balance the cob on its blunt end, upright, hold it up with one hand, and cut down the cob. Others hold the cob with one hand, sideways, over a large bowl, and carefully slide the knife along the ear. The corn kernels will fall into the bowl. Whichever technique you use, be sure to use a sharp knife. You have to push harder to force a dull knife through the kernels, which means that the knife is more likely to slip.

INGREDIENTS:
2 medium tomatoes, cut in ¼-inch dice
1 medium red onion, cut in ¼-inch dice
1 red bell pepper, cut in ¼-inch dice
1 green bell pepper, cut in ¼-inch dice
2 garlic cloves, minced
½ cup cilantro, chopped and lightly packed
½ pound Swiss cheese, cut in ¼-inch dice
½ cup Parmesan cheese, grated
6 ears corn
1 teaspoon salt, or to taste
1 teaspoon black pepper, or to taste
1 cup extra virgin olive oil

PREPARATION:

Prepare the tomatoes, onion, peppers, garlic, and cilantro per the ingredient list. Dice the Swiss cheese; grate the Parmesan cheese if you aren't using pre-grated cheese.

Bring a large pot of water to boil over high heat. Remove the husk and silk from the corn, submerge in the boiling water and cook for 8 minutes. Plunge the ears in cold water, to stop the cooking, and drain.

With a sharp knife or a corn stripper, cut the corn kernels from the cobs. Put the cut corn in a large mixing bowl and add the chopped tomatoes, onion, peppers, garlic, cilantro, and cheeses. Mix lightly. Add salt and pepper to taste. Pour the olive oil over the salad and toss lightly. Let the salad sit for 30 minutes before serving, so that the flavors can blend.

Sweet Potato-Crusted Kona Kampachi with Tomato-Papaya Coulis
SERVES 4

Okinawan or purple sweet potatoes grow very well in the deep soils along the Hāmākua coastline; they are a major agricultural product of the Big Island. In 2008, over 10 million pounds of purple sweet potatoes were grown on the Big Island; some were consumed here, and the rest were shipped to all parts of the world. The continental US has recently discovered this wonderful Big Island product and the demand has been growing year by year.

One cup of Okinawan purple sweet potato contains 140 calories, 4 grams dietary fiber, 29 mg calcium, 271 mg potassium, 30 mg vitamin C, and 18 mcg folate. It is rich in antioxidants, which help prevent cardiovascular disease and cancer. No wonder Okinawa, where this wonder crop was developed, is home to a world-record number of senior citizens over 100 years of age!

Chef Neil Murphy of Merriman's Restaurant developed this tour-de-force recipe for sweet potato-crusted Kona kampachi. It uses not only our Big Island sweet potatoes, but also the Kona kampachi raised at the NELHA facility near Kailua-Kona.

INGREDIENTS:
4 (4 ounce) Kona kampachi fillets, skinless and boneless
3 medium-size purple sweet potatoes
¼ cup canola oil
Sea salt and pepper to taste

For the coulis:
½ onion, cut in ⅛-inch dice
1 clove garlic, finely minced
2 ripe tomatoes, cut in ⅛-inch dice
½ ripe, but firm papaya, cut in ½-inch dice or chunks
2 tablespoons fresh basil, chopped
4 tablespoons olive oil
Salt and pepper to taste

For the garnish:
Lemon wedges
Fresh basil leaves

To prepare the coulis: Cut up the onion, garlic, tomatoes, papaya, and basil per the ingredients list. Heat the olive oil in a saucepan over medium heat. Add onions and garlic and cook till the onions

are translucent. The onions should not brown. You are sweating, not sautéing them. Add the tomatoes and papaya and cook on medium heat for 15 minutes. Remove from heat, purée in a food processor, blender, or food mill, strain to remove lumps, and season to taste with salt and pepper. Top the finished coulis with the chopped basil.

To prepare the potatoes and fish: Peel the sweet potatoes and shred them; a mandolin works well for this, if you have one. Rinse the shredded potatoes in warm water.

Place some shredded potatoes on a large plate, put the fish fillets on top of the potatoes, and sprinkle another layer of shredded potatoes over the fish.

Put the ¼ cup oil in a non-stick sauté pan over medium heat. When the oil is hot, carefully slide the layered potato and fish into the pan. When one side of the fillets turns crispy and somewhat brown, turn the fillets over and crisp the other side. Remove from pan and season with salt and pepper.

PRESENTATION:

For individual servings, arrange one fillet on a plate, make a puddle of coulis on side and garnish with basil leaf and a lemon wedge. To serve family style, arrange the fillets on a platter and drizzle a ribbon of coulis around the fish. Garnish and serve.

'Ōhelo Berry Baked Brie
MAKES 2 CUPS

The 'ōhelo bush is native to the Islands; it is related to the blueberries and cranberries of the North American mainland. The 'ōhelo grows well at high altitudes and on the broken lands left by lava flows; it's a common sight around Volcano, where I live.

Its tart but sweet berries feature in many Island recipes. I find it a delicious accompaniment to cheese. Here's my recipe for 'ōhelo-berry baked brie. If you already have 'ōhelo-berry sauce sitting in the refrigerator (as I usually do), this recipe is a breeze.

INGREDIENTS:

For the 'ōhelo-berry sauce:
2 cups fresh 'ōhelo berries
1 cup sugar
1 cup white wine
¼ teaspoon salt, or to taste
2 tablespoons tapioca

For the 'ōhelo-berry baked brie:
⅓ cup 'ōhelo berry sauce
2 tablespoons brown sugar
1 ounce rum
⅛ teaspoon ground nutmeg
1 (8 ounce) round of Brie cheese
2 tablespoons chopped roasted macadamia nuts

PREPARATION:

To prepare the 'ōhelo sauce: Combine all ingredients in a saucepan, bring to a boil, and boil for 3 minutes, stirring constantly. Remove from heat and cool. Store in a covered container, refrigerated.

To prepare the baked brie: Pre-heat the oven to 500°F. Combine the 'ōhelo-berry sauce, sugar, rum, and nutmeg in a small bowl. Put the Brie in an over-proof dish and peel off the top rind. Top the Brie with berry sauce and sprinkle with the chopped macadamia nuts. Bake the dish of Brie in the pre-heated oven for 7 minutes, until the cheese is just warmed. Serve immediately, with crackers.

Fresh Poi

The Big Island supplies about 25 percent of the taro consumed in the State of Hawai'i. If you'd like to try making your own, you can usually find taro tubers at the local farmers' markets. The East Hawai'i markets are the most likely to carry them. I buy my taro and ginger from farmer Cyrus Wagatsuma.

There is nothing like fresh poi. I don't usually care for poi, but I love it when it's fresh!

Note that raw taro contains crystal needles of calcium oxalate that irritate the skin and throat if not cooked thoroughly. That is why it is important to thoroughly cook the taro; cooking dissolves the crystals. Also note that you'll need a scale to weigh the taro pieces and the portions of cooked taro.

INGREDIENTS:
Raw taro corms

PREPARATION:

Thoroughly wash taro. Put in a bucket or basin, cover with clean water, and soak overnight. This helps remove any dirt left on the corm.

Rinse the taro and cut into pieces weighing less than one pound. You may want to use gloves when you do this, as raw taro could make your hands itch. Steam the cut-up corms in a pressure cooker for 30 minutes, until they are easily pierced with a fork. If you aren't sure that they're done, cook a little longer; overcooking is better than undercooking when it comes to taro.

Remove the skin of the cooked taro and divide it into 5-ounce portions. What you do not use can be frozen for later use.

To make ½ pound of poi, coarsely grate 5 ounces cooked taro. Put the grated taro in a blender or food processor, add 4 to 5 tablespoons of boiling water, and blend. You may need to add more water (up to 3 to 4 more tablespoons) to get the right consistency.

Pour the fresh poi into a clean container. Cover and keep at room temperature until the poi naturally ferments to just the right degree. Some people like sweet-tasting one-day poi, others like their poi several days old, sharp and tangy.

Refrigerate the poi once fermented. Any poi that is in contact with air will dry out. You may want to store the poi in plastic bags, or put a layer of plastic wrap over the poi, or even add a thin layer of water atop the poi.

Hai Kou Veloute Soup
SERVES 4

Eva Lee, of Tea Hawai'i & Company, has also been experimenting in the kitchen, with recipes that make unconventional use of her Volcano green tea. If you happen to visit Volcano, you might want to buy some fresh tea from Eva, take it home, and try out her recipes. I think you'll be surprised, and then pleased, with these novel tastes.

This recipe is named after Eva Lee's grandmother, Nai Nai.

If you're not going to make this dish immediately, store the fresh tea sprigs in the refrigerator. They wilt rapidly.

INGREDIENTS:
- 4 freshly-plucked sprigs from a tea plant
- ¼ cup fresh tea leaves, finely-chopped
- 4 heaping tablespoons whole Volcano 'ōhelo berries
- 8 ounces sour cream
- 2 medium-size acorn squash
- 2 medium-size Yukon gold potatoes
- ½ medium-size Maui onion
- 1 cup rice milk
- ½ teaspoon powdered ginger
- Dash 'alaea salt
- ½ teaspoon cayenne pepper, or to taste

PREPARATION:

Stir the finely-chopped fresh tea leaves, whole 'ōhelo berries, and sour cream together. Chill in refrigerator.

Peel the squash, potatoes, and onion, and cut into ½-inch chunks. Put the cut-up vegetables in a saucepan, add water to cover, and bring to a boil. Turn the heat to low and add the rice milk, powdered ginger, alaea salt, and cayenne pepper. Simmer for one hour. Blend the soup in a blender or using an immersion (stick) blender.

PRESENTATION:

Ladle soup into 4 bowls. Add a heaping tablespoon of the tea leaf and berry mixture to each bowl. Top with fresh tea sprigs.

Tea Leaf Pesto
MAKES ½ CUP PESTO

For several decades, local farmers and agricultural scientists have experimented with growing tea on the Big Island. Their efforts are finally showing results, as Big Island tea makes its way to market and gains a reputation for taste and consistent quality.

Eva's tea pesto is great over pasta!

INGREDIENTS:

2 cups fresh tea leaves
½ cup freshly grated Parmigiano-Reggiano or Romano cheese
⅓ cup macadamia nuts, chopped
2 medium sized garlic cloves, minced
½ cup extra virgin olive oil
Salt to taste
Sugar to taste

PREPARATION:

Rinse the tea leaves, grate the cheese, chop the nuts, and mince the garlic.

Put all ingredients into a food processor and blend into a paste. The paste will keep in the refrigerator for weeks.

Aquacultural Industry

Aquaculture is one of Hawai'i's growth industries. It currently earns over 21 million dollars a year, and boasts a 19 percent annual growth rate. The Big Island is home to several branches of the industry.

The biggest is the Natural Energy Lab of Hawai'i Authority, or NELHA. It was created to explore the energy potential of the deep, cold waters off the Kona Coast, but is perhaps better known for the aquaculture firms that rent space in its Kailua-Kona facility. NELHA-based companies are raising popular foods such as seaweed, abalone, lobsters, moi, and kampachi.

Farmers on the Hāmākua coast are experimenting with aquaculture on a smaller scale, and the State Department of Fisheries has been supporting the mullet fishery at the mouth of Hilo's Wailoa River.

This aquaculture bounty has been a boon to Big Island cooks. It's great to have a ready supply of local, sustainably harvested seafood, and it's even greater that all this food is so very 'ono—as the following recipes will prove.

Big Island Baby Abalone Scampi
SERVES 8 AS AN APPETIZER

Chef de Cuisine Ed Mizuno of the Mauna Lani Bay Hotel and Bungalows is very pleased with the abalone he buys from the Big Island Abalone Corporation at Keāhole Point. KTA also carries Big Island abalone on the first Saturday of each month. Additionally, there is an abalone vendor at the Hilo Farmers Market. Chef Mizuno's developed several tasty abalone recipes to showcase the local delicacy. Here's one.

This recipe calls for clarified butter. Clarified butter is made by melting butter and letting it cook until the fat rises to the top of the pan and the milk solids settle to the bottom. The surface fat, or clarified butter, is skimmed off, leaving the unwanted solids behind. You can make your own clarified butter, or you can buy it from health food stores or Indian groceries, where it is sold under the name "ghee." Clarified butter has a higher smoke point than plain butter ... that is, you can heat it to a higher temperature before it starts to smoke. That makes it useful for sautéing.

INGREDIENTS:
   1½ pounds baby abalone (about
      16 to 24 abalone), shell intact
   ⅓ cup clarified butter (ghee)
   4 tablespoons minced garlic
   6 green onions, thinly sliced
   ¼ cup dry white wine
   2 tablespoons fresh lemon juice

For the garnish:
   2 tablespoons chopped fresh
      Italian parsley
   Parsely sprigs (optional)
   Lemon slices (optional)

PREPARATION:
Carefully rinse the baby abalone and set aside. Heat the butter in a large frying pan over medium heat. Cook the garlic 1 to 2 minutes, or until softened but not browned. Add abalone, green onion, wine, and lemon juice. The abalone should be placed flesh down, shell side up, and cooked for 1 to 2 minutes. Turn the abalone and cook the shell side for another 30 seconds. Do not overcook.

PRESENTATION:
Arrange the cooked abalone on a platter or individual plates. Salt and pepper to taste. Sprinkle with the chopped parsley and garnish with lemon slices and parsley sprigs, if desired.

Steamed Mullet with Salted Black Beans
SERVES 3

The State Fisheries Department operates a mullet hatchery on the Wailoa River. The mullet are thriving, once released, and fishermen are reeling in bountiful catches. This Chinese dish makes wonderful use of that fresh mullet.

This dish is cooked in a tiered steamer. If you don't already have one, you can buy traditional bamboo steamers that fit in a wok (these are usually quite inexpensive) or you can buy one of the many brands of stainless-steel tiered steamers. Tiered steamers are standard household equipment in many Asian countries. If you don't want to buy a steamer just for this dish, you can make an improvised one with a large covered pot and a stand or rack that fits inside the pot.

INGREDIENTS:
- 1 tablespoon soy sauce
- 3 tablespoons salted black beans or dau see, washed and mashed
- 1 large stalk green onion, chopped (should have at least 3 leaves)
- 1 (1-inch wide and 2-inches long) piece ginger, peeled and chopped
- ¼ cup cilantro, for garnish
- 3 medium sized mullet, scaled and gutted
- 1 teaspoon salt
- 1 tablespoon canola oil
- 1 tablespoon whisky
- ½ teaspoon sugar

For the constarch slurry:
- 1 tablespoon cornstarch
- 2 tablespoons cold water

PREPARATION:
Prepare the black beans, green onions, and ginger per the ingredient list. Wash the cilantro and pluck off the leaves, discarding the thickest stems.

Place fish in a bowl or pan that fits into your tiered steamer. Add the soy sauce, black beans, green onion, ginger, salt, oil, whisky, and sugar to a small bowl and mix well. Pour this sauce over the fish and put the pan of fish in the steamer.

Steam the fish for 20 minutes, or until fish is cooked (it will flake easily). Remove the pan and drain the liquids into a small pan. Mix the cornstarch and cold water in a small bowl or cup; make sure that there are no lumps. Add the cornstarch slurry to the pan full of cooking liquid. Heat the pan over low heat, stirring frequently, until the sauce thickens.

PRESENTATION:
Transfer the cooked fish to a serving platter and pour the thickened sauce over the fish. Garnish with cilantro.

Kona Kampachi Carpaccio with Ānuenue Hōʻiʻo Ogo Relish and Ginger Ponzu Sauce

SERVES 8 TO 10

Recently, the Hawaiʻi Visitors and Convention Bureau sponsored a series of mainland media events called "A Thousand Reasons to Smile." Island chefs ʻŌlelo Paʻa Faith Ogawa of Glow Hawaiʻi and Neil Murphy of Merriman's Restaurants ably represented the Big Island, giving cooking demonstrations that used products grown on the Big Island. Speaking to reporters, Chef Neil said, "The farmers make me look good with the outstanding products that they grow."

Chef Neil Murphy showcased NELHA-grown Kona kampachi with this wonderful carpaccio. Carpaccio is somewhat like sashimi, in that the fish (or meat) is served raw, but it is sliced very thin and served with a spicy Western-style sauce.

INGREDIENTS:

- 2 pounds fresh filet of Kona kampachi, sliced thin
- Shichimi togarashi (Japanese red pepper mix)
- 10 fresh shiso leaves, thinly sliced
- Fresh red radish, thinly sliced (optional)

For Ānuenue hōʻiʻo ogo relish with soy chili ginger
sauce:

- 1 bunch fresh hōʻiʻo fern shoots (warabi), blanched and cooled, then cut into ¼-inch pieces
- ½ medium diced sweet Maui onions (¼-inch dice)
- 1 diced Japanese cucumber (¼-inch dice)
- ½ diced red bell pepper (¼-inch dice)
- ¼ cup diced yellow bell pepper (¼-inch dice)
- ¼ cup chopped pickled ginger (¼-inch pieces)
- 1 medium diced tomatoes, (¼-inch dice)
- ½ cup chopped ogo (¼-inch pieces)

For the ginger ponzu sauce:
- ⅔ cup soy sauce
- ⅓ cup mirin
- ⅓ cup fresh lemon juice
- 1 tablespoon sugar
- 2 tablespoons peeled and minced fresh ginger
- Fresh Hawaiian chili pepper, to taste

PREPARATION:

To prepare the fish: Slice the fish as thin as you can. Slice the shisho leaves and the radishes, if you are using the radishes.

To prepare the relish: Chop all the ingredients per the ingredients list. Mix all ingredients together in a small bowl. Set aside.

To prepare the sauce: Prepare the ginger and chili pepper per the ingredients lists. Mix all ingredients and keep chilled until ready to use.

PRESENTATION:

Arrange the slices of kampachi carpaccio in a circle or oval around the edge of a serving platter. Sprinkle with shichimi tagarashi, shiso leaves, and sliced radish. Mound the relish in the center of the platter. Drizzle ponzu sauce over the dish. Serve immediately.

Kaffir Lime-Poached Kona Kampachi and 'Ahi
SERVES 4

Thepthikona "TK" Keosavang, the Chef de Cuisine at
Brown's Beach House, uses local ingredients to prepare
this wonderful dish, a tasty fusion of sophisticated Thai
cuisine and Western cooking.

Many of the ingredients—the kaffir lime leaves, lemongrass, Hawaiian chilies, ginger, scallions, organic watercress, organic micro-greens, and Kona Kampachi—
are grown or produced right here on the Big Island.

TK usually serves this fish with the soba salad recipe
that follows. You can make just the fish, or just the salad, if you'd like. You'll lose something of the complexity
and sophistication of the restaurant presentation, but
you may find that the abbreviated versions work better for you.

Truffle oil sounds like an expensive ingredient, but it doesn't cost much more than a good
virgin olive oil. In fact, that's basically what it is: a good olive oil flavored with thioether, an
organic compound found in truffles. If you don't want to buy truffle oil just for this recipe,
you can substitute a high-quality olive oil.

TK likes to garnish the dish with organic micro-greens. These are greens and herbs that
have just started to grow; they are tender and delicious. If you can't find micro-greens, or
can't afford them, use your favorite herbs or greens, finely cut.

The chili oil and the truffle-soy dressing are good in themselves. If you like them, you may
want to make larger amounts and store for later use.

INGREDIENTS:
- 1 (8 ounce) center-cut Kona kampachi fillet
- 1 (8 ounce) center-cut sashimi-grade 'ahi fillet
- 2 quarts of court-bouillon (see recipe on next page)
- ½ cup sweet chili oil (see recipe on next page)
- ½ cup lemon truffle soy dressing (see recipe on next page)
- ½ cup organic micro-greens, for garnish
- ¼ cup organic watercress, for garnish

For the court-bouillon:
4 lemongrass stalks (smashed)
½ cup peeled and crushed ginger
12 kaffir lime leaves
1 x 2-inch piece kombu
3 Hawaiian chilies
4 cups water
½ cup sake
2 tablespoons Hawaiian sea salt

For the sweet chili oil:
2 tablespoons grape seed oil
1 teaspoon sugar
1 teaspoon paprika
1 teaspoon cayenne

For the lemon truffle soy dressing:
2 tablespoons Yamasa soy sauce
1 tablespoon truffle oil
1 tablespoon yuzu juice
1 tablespoon peeled and grated fresh young ginger
1 tablespoon finely-chopped toasted garlic
1 tablespoon grapeseed oil

PREPARATION:

To prepare the sweet chili oil: Combine all the listed ingredients in a saucepan and bring to a simmer. Let the oil cool. Pour the cooled oil through a coffee filter, to remove any solid ingredients. Put in a closed container and store until ready to use. This can be done the day before you plan to cook the fish.

To prepare the lemon truffle soy dressing: Toast the garlic by removing the papery covering on several garlic cloves (enough to make 1 tablespoon). Do not peel the cloves. Heat a small frying pan over medium heat and put the garlic cloves in the pan. Watch carefully and stir them frequently. Cook until they are golden brown; this should take only a few minutes. Remove from the heat, cool, peel, and chop. Combine the soy sauce, truffle oil, yuzu juice, ginger, garlic, and grapeseed oil in a mixing bowl. Mix well, taste, and correct the seasoning if desired. Put in a closed container and store until ready to use. Shake before using if if the oil has separated. This also can be done the day before you plan to cook the fish.

(recipe continued on page 70)

To prepare the court-bouillon:
Trim the lemongrass stalks, if necessary, and smash them with the flat of a heavy knife; this will release their flavor. Peel and crush the ginger, count out the kaffir lime leaves, and cut the piece of kombu. Remove the stems from the Hawaiian chilies. Put the 4 cups of water in a medium-size stockpot and add the prepared vegetables, the sake, and the salt. Bring to a simmer over medium heat and cook for 5 minutes.

You can prepare the court-bouillon just before poaching the fish. You can also make it ahead of time. To make ahead, strain it through a sieve into a container with a tight lid. Throw out the vegetables. Refrigerate (if using the next day) or freeze.

You can also reuse the court-bouillon after you have used it for poaching. Strain and add some water (about ⅔ cup of water to 1 quart of bouillon) to make up for the water lost in the poaching. Freeze and save to use again.

TO POACH THE KAMPACHI AND 'AHI:

bring the court bouillon to a rolling boil, then turn the heat down to low. Let the boil subside. Submerge the fish in the court-bouillon for 15 seconds, then remove and cool.

Do not rinse the fish under cold running water or submerge in ice water to speed the cooling; let the fish cool gradually. This will preserve the flavor. Cover and put in the refrigerator to chill. Just before serving, cut each fillet into thin slices.

PRESENTATION:

Arrange the slices of kampachi and 'ahi on a serving platter or on individual plates. Drizzle the fish with chili oil and truffle-soy dressing, and garnish with Hilo organic watercress and Kona micro-greens.

Soba Salad
SERVES 2

TK makes this salad to go with his wonderful Kaffir Lime-Poached Kona Kampachi and 'Ahi (see page 68). However, it's great without the fish.

INGREDIENTS:
½ pound soba noodles, cooked
¼ cup julienne carrot
2 tablespoons green onion, cut into thin slices on the diagonal
2 tablespoons slivered Maui onion
¼ teaspoon toasted black and white sesame seeds
1 cup sesame soy vinaigrette (see below)

For the sesame-soy vinaigrette:
2 tablespoons Yamasa soy sauce
2 tablespoons yuzu juice
2 tablespoons brown sugar
2 tablespoons Dijon mustard
1 tablespoon Sriracha chili sauce
2 tablespoons sesame paste (tahini)
1 cup grapeseed oil
White pepper to taste
Salt to taste

PREPARATION:

To prepare the vinaigrette: Combine the soy sauce, yuzu, brown sugar, Dijon, Sriracha, and sesame paste in a blender. While the blender is running, pour a thin trickle of oil through the hole in the lid. The oil and the spice paste will emulsify, making a smooth dressing. Season with salt and pepper to taste. Put in a closed container and store until ready to use. Shake before using if the oil has separated. You can do this a day or more ahead of time.

To prepare the soba: At least one hour before you plan to serve the salad, cook the noodles per the package directions. Drain, rinse, and put the noodles in the refrigerator to chill.

While the noodles are chilling, peel and julienne the carrot; cut the green onion into thin slices on the diagonal (not straight across). Cut the sweet onion into small julienne strips (slivers). Gently mix the cooked noodles, the prepared vegetables, the sesame seeds, and the sesame soy vinaigrette.

'Ahi Katsu Burger
MAKES 14 (6-OUNCE) PATTIES

Big Island fishermen bring in some of the finest 'ahi to be found. During the summer, when the seas are calm, you can find 'ahi chunks in KTA's fish section for as little as $1.99–$3.99 per pound. That is when Big Islanders indulge in all sort of tasty 'ahi dishes—such as this spicy 'ahi burger from Sous-chef Bryceson Velez of the Mauna Lani Bay Hotel and Bungalows.

This is a big picnic, potluck, or lū'au-size recipe. Feel free to cut it in half if you're making it for a smaller gathering.

INGREDIENTS:

For the patties:
5 pounds chopped or ground fresh 'ahi (you can use the smaller, less expensive smaller 'ahi chunks)
½ cup minced round onion
¼ cup sliced green onion
½ tablespoon peeled and minced ginger
⅓ cup oyster sauce
½ tablespoon Sriracha chili sauce (or to taste)
2 teaspoons sesame oil
Panko bread crumbs (enough to coat the patties)
Oil for frying

For the Sriracha-tobiko aioli:
4 cups mayonnaise
½ cup Sriracha chili sauce
2 to 3 tablespoons fresh lemon juice (juice of 1 lemon)
¼ cup rice vinegar
1 tablespoon soy sauce
¼ cup tobiko (orange roe from the flying fish)
¼ cup sesame oil

PREPARATION:

To prepare the aioli: Measure the mayonnaise, Sriracha, lemon juice, vinegar, soy sauce, and tobiko into a blender and purée. With the blender running, pour a thin stream of sesame oil into the mixture, to emulsify the dressing.

(recipe continued on page 74)

To prepare the patties: Chop the 'ahi, the onions, and the ginger. Put in a large bowl and add the oyster sauce, chili sauce, and sesame oil. Mix well.

Heat a little oil in a frying pan over medium-high heat. Form one small patty and fry. Taste the patty and, if necessary, correct the seasoning in the patty mix. Hand-form 6 ounce patties and coat them in the panko bread crumbs. Fry the patties on both sides until crisp outside but still tender inside. Serve with Sriracha-tobiko aioli sauce or your favorite spicy mayonnaise-based sauce.

1/11/2012 mahalo Party; 1/4 recipe mini size
9/2023 D, mu

Crispy Moi and Cilantro Ginger Pesto
SERVES 2

Hilo Yacht Club is a private club in Hilo. The shoreline in front of the club is shallow and rocky; no boat, not even a dinghy, could anchor there. Members go to the club for the great view of the ocean, to watch the whales jumping from January till April, and to enjoy the club's great food.

Here is a recipe for local, farm-raised moi from Chef Ron Nahalea of the Hilo Yacht Club. It's quick and easy, but oh so 'ono.

INGREDIENTS:
1 fresh, cleaned moi (about 12 inches long, may weigh up to 1 pound)
Salt and pepper, to season fish
¼ cup cornstarch, for dredging fish
½ cup canola oil, for deep frying

For the cilantro ginger pesto:
¼ cup chopped macadamia nuts
½ cup fresh cilantro leaves, packed slightly
1 (2-inch) piece fresh ginger, peeled, chopped coarsely
1 cup canola oil

PREPARATION:

Combine the macadamia nuts, cilantro, and ginger in a food processor and purée until minced fine. Add the canola oil and mix again. Put in a microwavable container.

Cut 3 to 4 shallow slits on each side of the moi; season with salt and pepper, then dredge with cornstarch. Heat oil in deep frying pan and add the moi when oil is at 350°F. Cook the fish until it is crispy on one side, turn and fry the other side.

PRESENTATION:

Warm the pesto in the microwave. Place the crispy moi on a serving platter and pour warmed pesto sauce over the fish. Serve with steamed white rice. Enjoy!

Kona Cold Lobster Salad with Kona Mango Dressing
SERVES 2

Kona Cold Lobster, owned by Joe Wilson and located in Keahole, Kona, raises Maine lobsters in fresh, cold sea-water pumped up from deep offshore. The lobsters are sold when they reach about 1½ pounds. There is nothing like fresh lobster from the Big Island!

This very simple recipe tastes best when it is made with Big Island greens and tomatoes as well.

INGREDIENTS:

2 Kona Cold lobsters, 1½pounds each, cooked, then cooled
1 cup Big Island mixed greens
1 Big Island tomato, sliced

For the Kona mango dressing:
1 cup peeled and sliced mango
½ teaspoon fresh basil
½ teaspoon mint leaves
½ teaspoon fresh thyme
½ teaspoon chopped chives
1 teaspoon black peppercorns
½ cup white wine vinegar
½ cup honey
2 cups canola oil
Salt and pepper to taste

PREPARATION:

To prepare the mango dressing: Peel and slice the mango. Put the mango, herbs, peppercorns, vinegar, and honey into a blender or food processor and purée. With the machine running, add the oil in a thin stream. The dressing will emulsify. Add salt and pepper to taste.

To cook live lobsters: Bring a large pot of water to boil and put the lobsters, head down, into the pot. Remove the lobsters as soon as they turn red. Crack open the lobster tail and claws and remove the meat. Slice the tail meat.

Wash the greens and tomato; trim and slice the tomato.

PRESENTATION:

Arrange the greens and sliced tomato attractively on a plate. Fan the lobster meat over the greens. Drizzle some of the mango dressing over the lobster and greens.

Note: if you don't happen to have all four fresh herbs on hand, you can replace the basil, mint, thyme, and chives with dried or freeze-dried versions of the same herbs. Dried herbs are stronger, so you'd want to use half the quantity indicated—or less. Add the herbs a pinch at a time, crumbling the leaves between your fingers to bring out the flavor. Taste as you go. If your herbs are old and dried out, they may not be adding much flavor.

'Ele'ele Tsukudani
SERVES 4 AS A SIDE DISH

Royal Hawaiian Sea Farms, located in NELHA's Keahole technology park, grows different types of seaweed. One of my favorites is 'ele'ele seaweed. It looks like fine green hair. It is closely related to the awa nori seaweed of Japanese cuisine.

Steve Katase, of Royal Hawaiian, shared this easy recipe for a tasty 'ele'ele tsukudani (tsukudani is a Japanese side dish marinated in soy sauce). It would complement many of our local-style meals.

INGREDIENTS:
¼ cup 'ele'ele seaweed
3 tablespoons sugar
2 tablespoons soy sauce
2 tablespoons toasted sesame seeds
Hawaiian chili pepper, seeds removed, chopped

PREPARATION:

Combine the sugar, soy sauce, and sesame seeds. Add chopped chili pepper, little by little, until the sauce is as hot as you want it to be. Mix in the seaweed and serve. No need to marinate first.

Ranching and Livestock Industry

Ranching has been a major Big Island industry since the 1800s. Early ranchers ran cattle and shipped hides and tallow; later ranchers shipped cows to slaughterhouses on O'ahu. Today the livestock business is more diversified. Ranchers raise veal as well as beef (Daleico Ranch sells Hawaiian red veal, from calves that haven't been penned) and Kahua Ranch raises Hawaiian lamb. The Big Island has the only two remaining dairies in the state: Botelho Hawai'i Enterprises, a.k.a. Cloverleaf Dairy, and Island Dairy in O'ōkala. There are also several small pig farms.

Much of our output is shipped off to Honolulu, but enough stays here that we can enjoy meat that is locally and humanely raised—not to mention better for us. Recent work at the Mealani UH Experiment Station in Kamuela has shown that Big Island grass-fed beef is leaner than feed-lot beef, and has higher levels of beta-carotene, vitamin E, and omega-3 fatty acids. The clincher? It tastes better too!

Spicy Thai Beef Salad
SERVES 4

Kuahiwi Ranch in Ka'ū is run by the Galimba family. This is one of their favorite ways to prepare their grass-fed beef. There is little actual cooking involved, but you'll be doing lots of chopping.

INGREDIENTS:

1 pound Big Island grass-fed sirloin steak
1 tablespoon Thai fish sauce (nam pla)
4 cups shredded Manoa lettuce or other local mixed greens
1 medium Big Island tomato, cut into 8 wedges, (approximately 1 cup)
½ cup peeled, seeded, and sliced Big Island cucumber (⅛-inch thick slices) (about ¼ cucumber)
8 mint leaves, chopped
⅓ cup chopped cilantro
¼ cup green onions (about 1 stalk)
¼ cup sliced onion (⅛-inch slices)
¼ cup sliced button mushrooms (about 3 mushrooms)

For the dressing:
2 teaspoons finely minced garlic (about 2 cloves)
1 tablespoon minced ginger (approximate yield of a 1½-inch piece)
3 tablespoons Thai fish sauce
1½ tablespoons chili oil
2 tablespoons lime juice
1 tablespoon sugar

PREPARATION:

To make the dressing: Peel and mince the garlic and ginger. Mix all ingredients and set aside.

To prepare the salad: Wash and chop the greens, tomato, cucumber, mint, parsley, and green onion per the instructions in the ingredient list. Peel and slice the onion. Wipe the mushrooms clean with a damp cloth and cut into thin slices.

Marinate the beef in fish sauce for 10 minutes. Grill the steak until done, approximately 5 minutes per side. Slice the steak into thin strips across the grain. Shred the lettuce into bite-sized pieces.

PRESENTATION:

Mound the lettuce or greens on a platter or in a large bowl. Arrange the tomato, cucumber, onions, mushrooms, and mint leaves over the lettuce. Arrange the beef slices on top of the salad. Garnish the salad with green onions and cilantro and serve the dressing on the side.

Vietnamese Pho
SERVES 6

Vietnamese rice noodle soup, or pho, is increasingly popular on the U.S. mainland and in the Islands. It's a one-bowl meal, perfect for breakfast, lunch, or dinner, full of tender meat and crisp, fresh vegetables. It's not only healthy, but broke da mout' good.

The secret to good pho is good broth—and the secret to good broth is good beef. Here's a pho recipe that takes full advantage of our wonderful Big Island grass-fed beef.

The recipe calls for fish sauce. There are many kinds of fish sauce; you should use Vietnamese fish sauce, or nuoc mam, if you can find it. If you can't, Thai nam pla can be substituted. It's not quite the same, but the taste will be acceptable.

It's a nice touch to serve the soup in pre-heated bowls. You can put your soup bowls in a warm oven or set them on a warming tray for a few minutes before serving.

This is not a quick-and-easy recipe. The broth must cook for 3 hours. Schedule this for a day when you can stay home and enjoy the cooking.

INGREDIENTS:
1 pound dried (¹/₁₆-inch wide) rice noodles
⅓ pound Big Island grass fed sirloin

For the broth:
5 pounds beef knuckle bones
2 pounds beef chuck, cut into 2-inch cubes
2 (3-inch) pieces ginger
2 round onions
¼ cup fish sauce
3 tablespoons sugar
10 whole star anise
6 whole cloves
1 tablespoon salt

For the Vietnamese vegetable platter:
3 green onions, cut into ¼-inch pieces
⅓ cup chopped cilantro
1 pound mung bean sprouts
10 sprigs Thai basil
1 jalapeño chili, de-stemmed, cut into thin rings
1 lime, cut into 6 wedges
Black pepper

PREPARATION:

To prepare the broth: Fill a large stock pot with 6 quarts of water and start heating the water over medium-high heat.

While the first pot is heating, place the beef knuckle bones and the chuck cubes in a second pot and add water to cover. Bring to a boil and boil the meat vigorously for 5 minutes. Using tongs, transfer the bones and chuck cubes to the pot with 6 quarts water. Discard the water from the other pot.

Turn the heat under the large stock pot to high. When the water comes to a boil, lower to a simmer. Skim any foam or fat from the surface of the liquid.

Cut the knobs of ginger in half lengthwise and bruise with a meat mallet or the flat of a heavy knife. Peel the round onion. For additional depth of flavor, roast the ginger and the onions over an open flame, with a kitchen blowtorch, or under a broiler until lightly charred on the outside.

Drop the onion and ginger into the stock pot and add the fish sauce and sugar. Simmer the broth until the beef chuck is tender, about 40 minutes. Remove one cube of chuck, rinse it in cold water, cut it into thin slices, and set it aside in a covered dish. Let the other pieces continue to cook in the broth for another 1½ hours.

Remove the dry papery covering from the garlic cloves, but do not peel them. Heat a small frying pan or pan over medium-high heat and add the cloves. Toast, stirring frequently, until they are slightly browned. Remove the garlic and add the whole anise cloves to the heated pan. Cook and stir for a minute or two, just long enough to bring out the fragrance.

Put the star anise and garlic in a spice bag or wrap them in a piece of cheesecloth and tie with string. Add to the simmering broth. Simmer the bag until the broth smells of anise and garlic; this should take about 30 minutes. Remove and discard the anise and onions.

Add salt to taste and continue to simmer for another 20 minutes.

To prepare the raw beef slices: Put the sirloin in the freezer. It should be slightly frozen, so that it is stiff enough to cut in thin slices. If it is frozen hard, you will not be able to cut it easily. If it does freeze hard, leave it out on the counter until it is soft enough to cut. With an extremely sharp knife, cut slices as thin as you can manage, paper-thin if possible. Set aside in a covered dish until ready to serve.

To prepare the vegetable platter: Wash, trim, and chop the vegetables as per the instructions in the ingredients list. Arrange on a serving platter.

(recipe continued on page 84)

To prepare the rice noodles: Soak the noodles in cold water for approximately 30 minutes. If you soak them too long, they will become mushy. Fill a large pot with water and heat to boiling. Dip the soaked noodles in the boiling water for 1 minute and remove immediately. Again, if they are cooked too long they will become mushy. If you have a large sieve, this will make the dipping process easier.

PRESENTATION:

Place the vegetable platter in the center of the table, where your family or guests can serve themselves.

In the kitchen, place a serving of cooked noodles in each individual soup bowl. Place a few slices of beef chuck and raw beef on top of the noodles. Bring the broth to a rolling boil. Ladle 2 cups of broth into into each bowl. The broth will cook the raw slices of beef instantly.

Bring the bowls to the table and let guests add garnishes and flavorings from the vegetable platter as they please.

Kahua Ranch Roast Beef with Béarnaise Sauce
MAKES 24 (5-OUNCE) SERVINGS

Kohala's Kahua Ranch has been feeding Islanders for close to a century. It was started in 1928 by Atherton Richards and his friend Ronald Von Holt. They chose a Hawaiian name, Kahua, which means "beginning," "source," or "foundation."

In the late 1980s the ranch split into two operations, Kahua Ranch and Ponoholo Ranch. Kahua Ranch is still family-owned: it is run by Atherton's nephew Monty Richards. He raises cattle and sheep on 8,500 acres.

Monty's wife, Phyllis, shares with us this simple recipe for tasty roast beef. It's simple enough that the quality of the beef is crucial.

Phyllis recommends that you NOT salt the meat; she finds that the salt dries the meat. If you usually salt your roasts, do give her method a try.

INGREDIENTS:
8 pounds well-marbled, boneless, Big Island grass-fed rib roast, at room temperature
Salt and pepper to taste

For the Béarnaise sauce (Makes 1½ cups):
1 cup (2 sticks) butter, softened
1 teaspoon fresh tarragon
1 teaspoon fresh chervil
¼ cup tarragon vinegar
¼ cup white wine
2 shallots
2 egg yolks
1 tablespoon water

Salt and pepper to taste

PREPARATION:
Preheat oven to 300°F. Place roast fat side up on a rack in a roasting pan. Place in oven and roast approximately 16 minutes per pound for rare and 18 minutes per pound for medium. For even greater control, insert a meat thermometer in the thickest part of the roast: it should register 140°F when the roast is cooked rare, 160°F when medium.

(recipe continued on page 86)

Prepare the sauce while the roast is cooking. Set the butter out on the counter to soften. Combine the tarragon, chervil, vinegar, and wine in a small saucepan and simmer over medium heat until the mixture is reduced to a paste. Cool slightly, then transfer the herb mixture to the top of a double boiler. Place the boiler top over, not in, water that is simmering but not at a hard boil.

Separate the eggs. You'll have two leftover egg whites, which you may want to use in baking. Add 1 tablespoon of water to the egg yolks and whisk or beat the mixture until it is light and fluffy. Add the eggs to the herb mixture in the boiler and whisk.

Gradually whisk the softened butter into the sauce. Start with approximately 5 tablespoons and whisk until the sauce thickens again. Beat in 5 more tablespoons butter and whisk until thickened. Add the last 6 tablespoons of butter. Season to taste with salt and pepper.

PRESENTATION:
Slice the roast and pass the sauce separately.

Kulana Foods Rib Eye Steaks with Roquefort Butter
SERVES 4

Chef Ed Kenney, chef/owner of two Honolulu restaurants (Town and Downtown), loves Kulana Foods rib eye steaks! He claims "they are so succulent and full of flavor that they require nothing more than a little Hawaiian salt, cracked pepper, and a hot barbecue grill. However, at Town we have found the sharp pungency of Roquefort cheese to be an ideal complement to the robust 'beefy' steaks."

INGREDIENTS:
4 (approximately 8 ounces each) rib eye steaks

For the Roquefort butter:
½ cup (1 stick) softened butter
1 medium-size clove garlic, minced fine
2 tablespoons minced shallots (⅛-inch dice)
2 tablespoons finely-chopped Italian flat leaf parsley
¼ cup crumbled Roquefort or other blue-veined cheese
1½ teaspoon Worcestershire sauce
Salt and pepper to taste

PREPARATION:

To prepare the sauce: Set the butter out to soften. Peel and mince the garlic and shallots. Chop the parsley and crumble the cheese.

Heat 1 teaspoon of butter in a pan set over medium heat; add the garlic and shallot and sweat them for 2 to 3 minutes. They should soften rather than brown. Remove from heat and cool.

Scrape the garlic and shallot into a bowl and add the rest of the butter, the parsley, the crumbled cheese, and the Worcestershire sauce. Mix well. Season to taste with salt and pepper.

To prepare the meat: Grill the steaks over hot coals to the desired degree of doneness (medium rare is recommended). Remove the steaks from the grill and immediately smear 1 to 2 tablespoons of Roquefort butter on the top of each steak.

PRESENTATION:

Chef Kenny likes to serve these steaks with Ma'o organic arugula and homemade French fries. You may prefer oshitashi and white rice; the choice of vegetable and starch is up to you.

Note that any leftover butter will keep in the refrigerator for up to 2 weeks. It is great over steamed vegetables. Try it with asparagus, broccoli, cauliflower, or green beans.

Filipino Stew
or Pochero with Eggplant Sauce
SERVES 6

In 1906, plantation owners began importing Filipino laborers to work on Big Island sugar plantations. Whenever possible, the men brought over wives and family, and slowly but surely, the Big Island Filipino community took shape. Filipinos have added their food, music, and culture to the local mixed plate, and we're all of us the richer for it.

Here's a recipe for beef pochero, an easy Filipino stew. This version of the dish calls for removing the beef and chorizo and serving them separately, with an eggplant sauce. If you are pressed for time, you may want to skip the eggplant sauce and leave the chunks of beef and sausage in the soup. The pochero is delicious either way.

INGREDIENTS:

For the first stage:
2 pounds Big Island stew meat or beef chuck, cut into 2-inch cubes
½ pound chorizo (Spanish sausage), cut into 1-inch rounds
½ bunch green onions, cut into 2-inch lengths
2 quarts water
1 tablespoon water
2 teaspoons salt
1 teaspoon black pepper

For the eggplant sauce:
3 medium-size round eggplants
2 cloves garlic, minced
¼ cup white vinegar
1 teaspoon salt
½ teaspoon black pepper

For the second stage:
1 medium-size onion, sliced in half then, sliced into ⅛-inch slices
2 cloves garlic, crushed
4 medium-size tomatoes, chopped into ¼-inch diced
1 teaspoon salt
½ pound long beans, cut into 2-inch lengths
1 small head Chinese cabbage, cut into 2-inch lengths
1 small head cabbage, cut into wedges
3 medium-size sweet potatoes, quartered
1 can (15 ounces) garbanzo beans OR 2 cups home-cooked beans)
¼ cup canola oil

PREPARATION:

To start the stew: Cut up the beef, chorizo, and green onions. Put them in a large stew pot, and add the 2 quarts of water, 2 teaspoons salt, and black pepper. Cover and bring to a boil; lower heat and keep at a low simmer for 2½ hours.

Prepare the eggplant sauce while the stew is simmering. Put the eggplants, unpeeled, in a large pot and cover with water. Boil until the eggplants are tender, which should take about 20 minutes. Peel them and cut them into chunks. Purée the chunks in a blender. Peel and mince the garlic; add the garlic, vinegar, salt, and pepper to the eggplant purée. Blend, taste, and correct the seasoning if necessary. Cover and set aside.

While the stew is still simmering, cut up the onion, tomatoes, beans, cabbage, sweet potatoes, and garlic per the ingredients list. Rinse and drain the canned garbanzo beans, if using canned beans.

When the stew has finished its 2½ hour simmer, remove the beef and chorizo from the pot, leaving only the broth. Put the beef and chorizo in a covered serving dish and keep warm.

In a large frying pan, heat the ¼ cup canola oil and sauté the garlic and onion. Add the cut tomatoes, garbanzo beans, and 1 teaspoon salt. Simmer for 10 minutes. Add these cooked vegetables to the pot of broth. Add long beans and Chinese cabbage, and bring the broth to a boil again. Add head cabbage and sweet potatoes and cook until tender, about 20 minutes.

(This process may seem unnecessarily complicated, but it's done for a reason; vegetables that require longer cooking are added first, and the ones that cook more quickly are added later. This ensures that the vegetables are soft, but not mushy.)

PRESENTATION:

Make sure that the beef and chorizo, and the eggplant sauce, are still warm. You may need to reheat them briefly in the microwave. Arrange the meats on a platter and serve the eggplant sauce on the side. Serve the vegetable soup in individual bowls or in a soup tureen.

Butterflied Leg of Lamb
SERVES 8 TO 10

Some Big Island ranches, such as Kahua Ranch, raise sheep as well as cattle. Locally raised lamb (leg of lamb, racks, and shoulders) is often available at local markets.

This grilled leg of lamb is always a hit at a party. It's super easy as well: marinate overnight, stuff, and roast.

INGREDIENTS:
1 (approximately 5 pounds) boneless leg of lamb
¾ cup dry red wine
⅓ cup fresh lemon juice
½ cup minced fresh basil leaves
2 tablespoons sugar
1 tablespoon fresh rosemary OR 2 teaspoons crumbled dried rosemary
1 tablespoon fresh oregano OR 2 teaspoons crumbled dried oregano
**   leaves**
1 large onion, for stuffing
2 large garlic cloves, thinly sliced, for stuffing
½ cup crumbled feta cheese, for stuffing
Basil and oregano leaves for garnish

PREPARATION:

Remove the lamb from the butcher's netting. Spread out, boned side up, and trim away the fat. Mix the wine, lemon juice, ½ cup basil leaves, sugar, rosemary leaves, and oregano in a large pan or bowl. Add the lamb to the bowl and turn it until it is thoroughly coated with the marinade. Cover the pan or bowl tightly and put in the refrigerator to marinate overnight.

The next day, peel the onion and cut it into ½-inch slices. Cut the slices in half so that you have onion half rounds. Peel and slice the garlic, and crumble the feta, if not already crumbled. Preheat the oven to 350°F.

Lift the meat from the marinade, reserving the liquid. Lay the meat flat, boned side up. Cut slits about ½-inch deep, and as wide as the onions, all over the meat. Fit the garlic slices into the slits. Fit the sliced onions, curved side out, into the slits that hold the garlic. Spread the crumbled feta cheese evenly over the lamb. Re-roll the lamb and secure the roll with kitchen twine.

Roast at 350°F for 1½ hours, or until the internal temperature reaches 155°F. The lamb should till be rare and the meat reddish. To my mind, this is the best way to eat lamb—be careful not to overcook it.

Kahua Ranch Kālua Lamb Shoulder
SERVES 8

Is kālua pork the only kind of kālua you can make? Certainly not! To kālua something just means to bake it in an imu, an earth oven. Island folks have learned to reproduce that great imu flavor with ti leaves, liquid smoke, and a few hours in an oven or slow cooker. You can kālua pork, beef, or, as in this recipe, Big Island lamb.

Merriman's Neil Murphy, one of the Big Island's top chefs, has come up with a great recipe for kālua lamb shoulder. It features not only our home-grown lamb, but coffee from our Kona coast.

INGREDIENTS:
2 pounds Kahua Ranch lamb shoulder, cut into large cubes
1 + 1 large round onions
2 tablespoons + 1 teaspoon canola oil
2 cups water or lamb stock
3 tablespoons Hawaiian red sea salt or Kona sea salt
1 ti leaf
2 tablespoons liquid smoke
1 large head cabbage
¾ cup grated white cheddar

For the coffee barbecue sauce:
1 cup fresh pineapple, peeled, eyes removed, and chopped coarsely
1 cup ketchup
1 cup brown sugar
¼ teaspoon ground cumin
¼ teaspoon liquid smoke
¼ cup rice vinegar
¼ cup sweet chili sauce
2 tablespoons fresh Kona coffee, fine grind

PREPARATION:

To prepare the sauce: Prepare the pineapple per the directions in the ingredients list. Place pineapple and all other sauce ingredients in a large saucepan and simmer for 20 minutes, till sauce is thickened. Cover and set aside.

To prepare the lamb: Preheat the oven to 300°F. Cut the lamb into chunks and coarsely chop only ONE of the onions. Sear the chunks of lamb in 2 tablespoons of canola oil in a cast-iron Dutch oven or lidded, enameled cast-iron casserole, set over medium-high or high heat. Turn off the heat and add the water, salt, chopped onion, and liquid smoke. Top with the ti leaf. Cover the pot and put into the preheated oven.

Cook the lamb for approximately 3 hours or until tender. Take the lamb out of the cooking pot and shred it with a fork. There should be about ¼ cup of cooking juices left in the pot. Don't throw these out! You'll use them later when you bake the lamb and cabbage rolls.

Peel the second onion. Slice it in halves and then into slices as thin as you can manage. Heat a frying pan over medium heat, add approximately 1 teaspoon of canola oil, and sweat the onion shreds until they are soft and translucent. They should not brown, just soften. Add the onion to the shredded lamb and mix well.

Grate the cheddar cheese and mix with the lamb and onion.

Remove the outer leaves and the center rib from the head cabbage. Poach in boiling salted water to cover, just until soft; this should take about 5 minutes. Remove the cabbage from the boiling water and plunge into a bowl of ice water. This will stop the cabbage from cooking further and becoming mushy. Place the cabbage leaves in a colander to drain.

If you turned off the oven while you were preparing the lamb mixture and the cabbage leaves, turn it on again and preheat to 350°F.

Spread one cabbage leaf flat on a cutting board, put 2 tablespoons lamb mixture in the center of the cabbage leaf, and roll the leaf into a 1-inch cylinder. Repeat until all the lamb mixture is used up.

Place the lamb and cabbage rolls in a buttered casserole dish, add the pan juices left over from baking the lamb. If you don't have a full ¼ cup, add water until you have ¼ cup. Bake in the preheated 350°F oven for 10 minutes.

PRESENTATION:

Place the lamb rolls on a serving platter and serve with coffee barbecue sauce. You can pool the sauce on the platter and put the rolls on top, drizzle sauce over the rolls, or serve the sauce on the side; it's up to you.

Carne de Vinha D'alhos Island Pork
SERVES 8 TO 10

When you buy local pork, you're supporting recycling. Our hard-working pig farmers pick up green waste and slop from local restaurants and markets, sterilize it, and feed it to their pigs.

Many local cuisines use this pork in tasty ways. One popular dish is Portuguese: pork marinated with spices and vinegar. It's both delicious and easy. No wonder it's a local favorite! Try serving this dish accompanied by the fried breadfruit on page 55.

INGREDIENTS:
- 4 pounds Big Island pork roast
- 2 teaspoons chopped Hawaiian chili pepper (about 2 peppers) or to taste
- 4 cloves garlic, minced
- 2 bay leaves
- 5 whole cloves
- ¼ teaspoon dried thyme
- ¼ teaspoon dried sage
- 1¼ cups cider vinegar
- 1 tablespoon salt

PREPARATION:

Chop the chili peppers and garlic. If you don't like hot food, you can use just one chili pepper. Mix the peppers, garlic, bay leaves, cloves, thyme, sage, vinegar and salt in a large pan or bowl. Add the pork roast and turn until it is covered with marinade. Cover the pan and refrigerate the pork. Marinate pork for 2 to 3 days; rotate the roast daily, to ensure even marination.

At the end of the marination period, drain the pork and dab it dry with paper towels. Place the roast in an ovenproof baking dish and cover it tightly with foil. Bake in a 375°F oven for 2¾ hours.

After the 2¾ hours, remove the foil and bake for another 15 minutes; this will allow the pork to brown. It's a good idea to check the roast with a meat thermometer at this point; the roast should be 150°F in the center. If it isn't, let it cook a little longer. When the roast is done, let the roast sit for 10 minutes before you slice and serve.

9/2023. P/ne

Willy Takaba's Favorite Beef Stroganoff
SERVES 4 TO 5

This recipe comes from my old classmate and friend, Willy and Cheryl Ann Takaba. Willy and Cheryl are true Hiloans: born in Hilo, went to Hilo High School. They went away to college, but came back here to marry and raise a family. Willy is currently Mayor Billy Kenoi's managing director.

This dish is the kind of food we were eating back in the '60s and '70s. It's not trendy, but it's tasty and satisfying. Give it a try.

INGREDIENTS:
- 1 pound sirloin, cut into ¼-inch strips
- 1 (3 ounce) can sliced mushrooms, drained
- ½ cup chopped onion (¼-inch dice)
- 1 clove garlic, minced
- 1 tablespoon flour
- ½ teaspoon salt
- 2 + 2 tablespoons butter
- 3 tablespoons flour
- 1 tablespoon tomato paste
- 1¼ cups beef stock
- 1 cup sour cream
- 2 tablespoons dry white wine

For the noodles:
- 2 cups cooked egg noodles
- Butter to taste

PREPARATION:

Cut the sirloin into strips as thin as you can manage. ¼-inch is good, thinner is better. Drain the mushrooms, peel and chop the onion, peel and mince the garlic.

The stroganoff cooks quickly once started, so it might be a good idea to cook the noodles per package directions at this point. Drain the noodles, butter, and set aside in a covered dish to keep warm.

Coat the sirloin strips with 1 tablespoon flour and ½ teaspoon salt. Heat 2 tablespoons of the butter in a frying pan over medium-high heat, Add the sirloin and brown the strips quickly. Add mushrooms, onion, and garlic. Cook 3 to 4 minutes or until the onion has softened a little. Remove the meat mixture from pan.

Turn the heat under the pan down to medium and add the remaining 2 tablespoons of butter to the pan drippings; mix well. Add the 3 tablespoons flour and whisk until you have a uniform flour paste, a roux. Whisk in the tomato paste.

Slowly add the beef stock, whisking as you pour. Cook and whisk until the sauce is thickened and bubbly.

Return the strips of cooked sirloin and the vegetables to the pan. Stir in sour cream and white wine. Cook slowly until evenly heated, do not boil.

PRESENTATION:

Serve the stroganoff over the buttered noodles.

1/3/2011 - David, me would make again.

Green Tea Panna Cotta
SERVES 4

There were once dairies on every island, but the high cost of land and imported feed forced most of them to close. The state of Hawai'i now gets most of its milk from the mainland. We Big Islanders are lucky to be able to buy truly fresh milk from the two remaining Island dairy farms, both on the Big Island: Island Dairy and Cloverleaf Dairy (a.k.a. Botelho Hawai'i Enterprises).

The following recipe combines fresh local milk and Big Island–grown green tea powder. This delicately flavored green tea panna cotta is both tasty and low fat.

It isn't a lot of work, but it does need to be chilled for at least 6 hours. You may want to make this treat the day before you plan to serve it.

INGREDIENTS:
- 2 teaspoons unflavored gelatin
- 2 tablespoons cold water
- 1½ cups whole Big Island milk
- 7 tablespoons sugar
- ⅛ teaspoon salt, or to taste
- 1½ cups low fat buttermilk
- 2 teaspoons Big Island green tea powder

PREPARATION:

Measure the 2 tablespoons of cold water into a small bowl and sprinkle the gelatin over the water. Let the gelatin mixture stand for 5 minutes, or until the gelatin softens.

In a medium saucepan, combine the milk, sugar, and salt and warm over moderate heat for about 3 minutes, stirring frequently to dissolve the sugar. Remove from heat, whisk in the gelatin mixture and whisk until completely dissolved. Add the buttermilk. Pour 1 cup of the panna cotta mixture into a microwaveable measuring cup, cover, and refrigerate until ready to use.

Pour another ¼ cup of the panna cotta mixture into a small bowl, add the green tea powder, and whisk until the powder has dissolved and is thoroughly mixed. Pour the tea-flavored panna cotta back into the panna cotta in the saucepan and whisk well. Pour the tea-flavored panna cotta into four (8 ounce) glasses and refrigerate until just set, about 3 hours.

Remove the reserved 1 cup of panna cotta from the refrigerator. Place it in your microwave and heat it for 15 seconds or so, until it softens enough to be pourable (it stiffens in the refrigerator).

Pour a layer of the plain panna cotta over the chilled, tea-flavored panna cotta in the glasses. Cover the glasses again and refrigerate them until the top layer of panna cotta is firm again; this will take at least 3 more hours.

Hawaiian Red Veal Italian Meatballs
SERVES 4 TO 6

Hawaiian red veal is a humanely raised, locally grown and processed veal produced by the Hawai'i Cattle Producers Cooperative Association and Kulana Foods of Hilo.

Traditionally raised veal comes from calves that have been separated from their mothers and confined to crates or hutches, where they are fed on processed milk products. Their meat is fat and pinkish-white. Red veal comes from 5- to 6-month-old calves that have been allowed to stay with their mothers until weaning; they have been free to roam and eat grass. Their meat is leaner and pinkish red.

Numerous consumers and restaurants have stopped buying traditionally raised veal and are turning to the red veal, which many believe to be less cruel. Top Island restaurants have joined this movement. Here on the Big Island, Merriman's Waimea, Mauna Kea Beach Resort, and Kona Village Resort serve Hawaiian red veal, when available.

This meatball recipe showcases the delicate taste of the red veal.

INGREDIENTS:
- ½ cup fresh bread crumbs
- ⅓ cup milk
- 1 pound ground Hawaiian red veal
- 2 tablespoons minced Italian parsley
- 2 medium garlic cloves, minced
- ½ cup grated Parmesan cheese
- 1 teaspoon salt
- Freshly ground black pepper

PREPARATION:

Place the bread crumbs and milk in a large bowl and soak for 10 minutes. Add the remaining ingredients and mix together well, kneading the mixture until it is smooth. (I use disposable gloves and mix by hand).

Pinch off a piece and cook it in a frying pan or in the microwave oven; taste and check the seasonings. Add more salt and pepper if needed.

(recipe continued on page 100)

With your hands, form meatballs, about 1 to 1½ inches in diameter. Place the meatballs on a plate or tray until you are ready to cook them.

Heat a large frying pan over medium heat. Add a little olive oil and when it is hot, add the meatballs. Brown the meatballs, frequently turning them in the pan. Cook the meatballs until they are well done. Remove from the pan.

PRESENTATION:

Serve them as appetizers or with a marinara sauce over pasta.

Slow Cooker Barbecued Beef
SERVES 4 TO 6

Too busy to cook? You can make this easy dish in a slow cooker. Put everything in the cooker when you get up, let it cook for an hour before you leave for work, turn it down and let it simmer all day. A hot meal will be waiting when you and your family get home.

Needless to say, this will taste much better if you make it with local grass-fed beef.

INGREDIENTS:
   1½ pounds Big Island chuck roast, cut into large chunks
   1 cup chopped onions (½-inch pieces)
   1 cup chopped green peppers (½-inch pieces)
   1 (6 ounce) can tomato paste
   ¼ cup packed brown sugar
   2 tablespoons cider vinegar
   1 tablespoon chili powder
   1 teaspoon Worcestershire sauce
   ½ teaspoon dry mustard
   1 teaspoon salt

PREPARATION:

Peel and chop the onions; trim, de-seed, and chop the green peppers. Put the roast on the bottom of a slow cooker or crockpot; add all the other ingredients. Do not stir. Cover and cook on high for one hour, then turn to low and cook for 8 to 10 hours, or until tender.

PRESENTATION:

Shred and serve on warmed buns with coleslaw. Also 'ono over freshly-cooked rice.

1/8/2011 Mahalo Party

Small Businesses

This chapter celebrates the many small businesses that supply the Big Island with healthy local foods and tasty treats. Some have been with us for several generations; some are new operations opened by hopeful strivers. I've singled out a few of the businesses that were willing to share their stories and their recipes. Does this reflect badly on the businesses not featured? Heavens, no! I wish I could make this chapter a lot longer than it is. So many treats, so few pages!

Emma's Green Salsa
MAKES 2 CUPS

Big Island Mexican Foods is the Big Island's largest source of locally made tortillas and salsas. Manual "Manny" Flores bought the Big Island Tortilla Company in 1996 and now sells his tortillas under the Mountain Apple Brand at KTA Super Stores and other markets and natural food stores around the island. You can also buy their products at their factory in the Shipman Industrial Park.

Just in front of the factory is a little restaurant called Emma's, where Emma treats her customers to some of her home-style Mexican dishes. Emma was willing to share the recipe for her special green salsa, served with her taquitos and tacos. This is one of my favorite salsas. A dollop of local avocado makes it wonderfully creamy and sweet.

INGREDIENTS:

½ cup avocado meat (about ½ of a medium Big Island avocado)
½ to 1 jalapeño pepper (to taste)
2 garlic cloves, crushed
½ medium sweet onion
1 pound (about 7) tomatillos
Salt and pepper to taste

PREPARATION:

Cut open the avocado, remove the pit, and spoon out ½ cup of the meat. Peel and crush the garlic cloves; trim and seed the jalapeño. Peel and coarsely chop the onion.

Bring a large pot full of water to a boil and turn off the heat. Remove the papery outer skin of the tomatillos, place in the water, and soak for 5 minutes.

Remove the tomatillos from the water and place in a blender with the avocado, garlic, and onion. Add only half of the jalapeño. Purée until smooth. Taste. Is it hot enough for you? If not, add the other half of the jalapeño and purée again. Remove from the blender, put into a serving bowl, and add salt and pepper to taste.

Serve with taquitos, tacos, and other Mexican dishes.

Madame Pele Truffles
MAKES 60 TRUFFLES

Melanie Boudar runs a thriving bed and breakfast, At the Crater's Edge, in Volcano. She recently branched out into another business, opening Sweet Paradise Chocolatier at the Kings' Shops in Waikoloa in 2009. She loves to cook, loves to make chocolates, and has turned her hobby into a business. She uses Hawaiian-grown chocolate whenever possible.

Here's one of her innovative recipes, which mixes the rich taste of chocolate with the fiery heat of Hawaiian chili peppers. That's why she calls them Madame Pele Truffles: they're hot! If you don't like that much heat, you can cut down the chili pepper slightly. If you overdid it on your first batch, just store them in the refrigerator and wait a week or so—the heat mellows over time.

(Many local folks have a chili pepper bush in the back yard; we harvest the peppers, dry them in a warm oven, and keep a bag of dried peppers on hand. For this recipe, you'd need to grind up some of those dried peppers. If you don't have a chili pepper bush or any dried peppers, you can use purchased cayenne powder.)

It can be tricky working with chocolate. Many recipes for chocolate candy call for careful melting in a double boiler, monitoring temperature with a candy thermometer, and careful stirring when the chocolate is cooling to temper it and keep it from seizing, turning dull and streaky. Melanie has developed a process that requires no tempering. If you've tried candy-making in the past and given it up as too difficult, try again. This recipe is practically foolproof.

INGREDIENTS:
8 ounces dark chocolate
8 ounces heavy whipping cream
¼ teaspoon ground cinnamon
½ teaspoon ground dried Hawaiian chili peppers or cayenne pepper

For the dusting powder:
¼ cup cocoa powder
1 cup confectioners sugar
¼ cup cinnamon sugar

PREPARATION:
Chop the chocolate into even-sized chunks, 1 to 2 inches or smaller.

Put the chocolate in a microwave-safe glass bowl and melt in the microwave. Set the timer for 30 seconds and the temperature to high. Repeat. Stir the chocolate. Heat for another 30 seconds. Altogether you will be heating the chocolate for 1½ minutes. The chocolate will not be completely melted.

Put the cream in a small saucepan and add cinnamon and ground chilies. Turn heat to medium-high and heat the cream to just below boiling. Pour the cream over the chocolate in the bowl and let the mixture sit for 1 to 2 minutes. Whisk the cream and chocolate until smooth; the mixture should have the consistency of mayonnaise. Pour mixture into an 8 x 8 inch baking pan and cover with plastic wrap. The wrap should be pressed down on the surface of the chocolate—otherwise a skin will form. Let the pan sit on the counter for 8 hours or overnight. (If it's much hotter than Hawai'i's usual 80 degrees, you may need to refrigerate the mixture.)

The mixture will crystallize. Scoop it out of the pan with a melon baller and roll into balls. Mix your dusting powder and roll the balls in the powder.

You can store the truffles in an airtight container for up to two weeks. They can be left on the counter if your kitchen isn't too hot. If you store them in the refrigerator, warm them to room temperature before serving.

Mehana Brewing Beer Batter Onion Rings
SERVES 6

Hilo's Shindo family started the Hilo Soda Works in the early 1950s. They used to sell their own orange, grape, strawberry, and cream sodas in glass bottles. Later they operated the Pepsi-Cola distributorship for the Big Island. In 1996, they made the jump to brewing beer, re-opening as the Mehana Brewing Company. The company started small and grew year by year. The successful company was recently acquired by Hawai'i Nui, d/b/a Keoki Beer.

Onion rings are a favorite brew-pub snack. Here is a recipe for onion rings that not only taste great with Mehana Red Ale, but are made with Mehana Red Ale.

INGREDIENTS:
2 medium-size sweet onions, peeled and sliced into ½-inch rounds
3 cups Mehana Red Ale beer
2 teaspoons apple cider vinegar
½ + ½ teaspoon salt
½ + ¼ teaspoon pepper
Canola oil for deep frying
¾ cup flour
¾ cup cornstarch
1 teaspoon baking powder

(recipe continued on page 106)

PREPARATION:

Peel and slice onions, place in large bowl, add 2 cups Mehana Red Ale beer, vinegar, ½ teaspoon salt, ½ teaspoon pepper. Refrigerate for at least 1 hour, but no longer than 2 hours.

Pur the canola oil into a large saucepan until it is 1-inch deep. Heat to 350°F (use a deep-frying thermometer to check the temperature).

While the oil is heating, combine the flour, cornstarch, baking powder, ½ teaspoon salt, and ¼ teaspoon pepper in a large bowl. Slowly whisk in ¾ cup beer until just combined. Do not over-mix. Over-mixing develops the gluten in the flour and makes the batter tough.

Drain the onion rings in a colander. Pat each ring with paper towels to dry. Dip a few rings into the batter and place them, one at a time, into the hot oil. Do not overcrowd! Flip the rings at least once, so that both sides are golden-brown and crisp. Drain the rings on paper towels. Season with salt and pepper.

You may find that you have a kitchen full of eager onion-ring eaters, happy to devour each batch as it comes out of the fryer. If you can make family and guests wait, transfer the drained and seasoned rings to a baking sheet in a 200°F oven, to keep warm until you have finished frying the whole batch and are ready to serve it.

Okara
MAKES 4 CUPS

Bean curd, or tofu, is made from soybeans. The beans are cooked, puréed, and filtered. The liquid that makes it through the filter is soymilk, which is coagulated to make tofu. The filtered-out soy pulp is called okara. It's not as popular as tofu, but it is cheap, nutritious, and tasty if properly prepared. I like to buy inexpensive tubs of raw okara from Oshiro Tofu, Natural Pacific Tofu, or Tomori Tofu Factory, located right here in Hilo. I use them to make this wonderful Japanese dish.

INGREDIENTS:
4 dried shiitake mushrooms
1 cup shredded Chinese cabbage
1 supermarket-size bunch green onions
¼ cup canola oil
1 pound okara
1 teaspoon hondashi
1 cup water
1 (4 ounce) package konnyaku (yam cake)

1 (2 ounce) package aburage
1 medium carrot, peeled
5 tablespoons sugar
1 tablespoon salt
1 tablespoon soy sauce

PREPARATION:

Soak the shiitake mushooms in hot water to soften them. Remove the stems and slice the mushrooms into julienne strips, ⅛-inch wide and 1-inch long. Set aside.

Set a few cups of water to boil in a small saucepan. Shred the Chinese cabbage and boil it for a minute or two. Drain and squeeze dry with your hands. It is important to remove as much water as you can; otherwise the cabbage will make the okara dish very soupy. Set aside.

Trim the green onions and cut into very thin slices

Heat the canola oil in a large frying pan or Dutch oven over medium-high heat. Add the okara. Cook, stirring constantly, until the okara is almost dry. Add the chopped green onions. Mix the hondashi with 1 cup water and add to the okara mixture. Lower the heat to medium and continue cooking until the okara is dry, or about 20 minutes. Stir frequently or the okara will burn.

In between bouts of stirring, cut up the konnyaku, aburage, and carrot. Slice them into julienne strips, ⅛-inch wide and 1-inch long, just like the shiitake mushrooms.

Add the konnyaku, aburage, carrot, shiitake, Chinese cabbage, sugar, salt, and soy sauce to the dry okara mixture and cook until the carrots are tender, about 25 minutes. Stir occasionally to mix and ensure even cooking.

PRESENTATION:

Serve over hot rice.

Hilo Coffee Mill's Barbecue Sauce

MAKES 6 CUPS

Hilo Coffee Mill operates a 24-acre farm just off Highway 11, at Mountain View.

The land was originally brought under cultivation as a coffee farm. In 1898, the Hilo side of the island had over 6,000 acres of coffee trees, planted from Pana'ewa up to Volcano. However, when sugar plantations proved more profitable, the coffee trees were cut down. Now that sugar cane is no longer grown here, small farmers are bringing back coffee.

Entrepreneurs Jeanette and Kathy started Hilo Coffee Mill in February 2001 and now have over 4,000 coffee trees, a roasting room, and a testing and retail area. They also tend many free-range chickens.

Some of these chickens end up on the barbecue grill, brushed with a special barbecue sauce made with the Coffee Mill's gourmet espresso coffee. I asked for the recipe and Jeanette kindly shared.

Note that this makes a large batch of barbecue sauce. However, it's so good that I bet you'll use it up in no time.

INGREDIENTS:

5¼ cups ketchup (1 (44 ounce) container of ketchup)
½ cup mustard
3 cups packed brown sugar
⅓ cup espresso coffee (about 2 shots)
1 (20 ounce) can crushed pineapple, with juice

PREPARATION:

Put all ingredients into a medium saucepan and cook over low heat for 20 minutes, stirring occasionally. It's as easy as that. Bottle and refrigerate until needed.

Brush over meat or poultry when you're grilling. Do this about 10 minutes before you expect the food to be done. If you brush on the sauce too early, it might burn.

Pipeline Porter Spice Cake
MAKES 1 (9 x 5½ INCH) LOAF OR ONE (8 X 8 INCH) SQUARE PAN

In 1995, the father-and-son team of Cameron Healy and Spoon Khalsa started the Kona Brewing Company. Their Kona plant brews Longboard Island Lager, Fire Rock Pale Ale, Pipeline Porter, and Wailua Wheat Ale. Their beer is distributed throughout the U.S. and Japan. They also operate two brew-pubs, one in Kona and one in Honolulu.

Beer can be an ingredient as well as a drink. For instance, it's commonly used in stews, such as Belgian beef stew. Here's an unusual use of beer: as an ingredient in a spice cake. The intensely flavorful dark porter complements the dried spices and fresh ginger. Sound crazy? Try it and see!

INGREDIENTS:

- 1 cup Kona Brewing Company Pipeline Porter
- 1 cup molasses
- 1½ teaspoons baking soda
- 3 large eggs
- ½ cup white sugar
- ½ cup dark brown sugar
- ¾ cup vegetable oil
- 2 cups flour
- 2 tablespoons ground ginger
- 1½ teaspoons baking powder
- ¾ teaspoon ground cinnamon
- ¼ teaspoon ground cloves
- ¼ teaspoon grated nutmeg
- ¼ teaspoon ground cardamom
- 1 tablespoon peeled and grated fresh ginger

PREPARATION:

Preheat oven to 350°F. Butter and flour a loaf pan or a 8 x 8 inch square pan.

In a large saucepan combine the Pipeline Porter and molasses and bring to a boil. Turn off the heat and add the baking soda. The mixture will foam up. Let it sit until the foam dissipates. In a separate bowl, whisk the eggs and sugars. Whisk in the oil. In yet another bowl, whisk together the flour, baking powder, and dried spices.

Combine the porter mixture with the egg mixture, then whisk the resulting liquid into the flour mixture. Add the freshly grated ginger and stir. Pour the batter into the prepared loaf pans and bake for 45 minutes to 1 hour, or until the top springs back when pressed.

Deli Roll Laulau
SERVES 6

Frank's Foods has been serving Hilo since 1954. This popular wholesaler sells Portuguese sausage, hot dogs, corned beef, and their special deli roll. When exiled Big Islanders return for a visit, they often buy Frank's deli roll to take home as an omiyage.

Here's an easy dish made with Frank's deli roll and local lū'au leaves. It's super simple: no need even salt! This is a big recipe, perfect for lū'au and potlucks.

You'll need a steamer to make this. Many local folks will have a three-tiered metal steamer pot. If you don't, you can buy an inexpensive bamboo steamer.

INGREDIENTS:
3 pounds Frank's Foods deli roll
25 lū'au leaves

PREPARATION:
Cut the deli roll into 3 x 1 inch slices. Wrap tightly in lū'au leaves; 1 large or 2 medium leaves per slice. Individually wrap in foil. Steam for 2½ hours on high. Check the water occasionally to make sure that the steamer doesn't boil dry. Serve while still hot and tasty. The rolls may taste greasy when cold.

Sakamoto Namul
MAKES 2 CUPS

My high school classmate, Arnold Sakamoto, raises mung bean sprouts, or moyashi. He sells them to KTA, under the Mountain Apple brand, and also to other Hilo markets.

There are always fresh bean sprouts in his kitchen. His wife likes to use them to make namul, a healthy and tasty Korean side dish.

INGREDIENTS:

½ cup soy sauce
⅓ cup salad oil
½ package dashi-no-moto
1 teaspoon sugar
3 to 4 garlic cloves, put through a garlic press
1 teaspoon sesame oil
Chili pepper to taste (optional)
1 package Mountain Apple Brand mung bean sprouts
¼ cup sliced green onions (about 2 stalks) for garnish

PRESENTATION:

Put the soy sauce, oil, dashi-no-moto, sugar, garlic, sesame oil, and optional chili pepper in a container with a tight-fitting lid. Shake the container until the dressing is emulsified.

Put the bean sprouts in a large bowl. Pour boiling water over the sprouts and let them soak for 5 minutes. Drain the sprouts and squeeze them gently with your hands to remove as much water as possible.

Put the drained moyashi into a serving bowl, add the dressing, and garnish with chopped green onions.

Bean Sprouts with Dried Shrimp
MAKES 4 (½ CUP) SERVINGS

Arnold also likes to eat his bean sprouts with dried shrimp. Here's a quick-and-easy shrimp dish that makes a great impromptu dinner.

INGREDIENTS:
- ¼ cup dried shrimp (ebi)
- 2 tablespoons butter
- 2 cups mung bean sprouts
- ½ teaspoon garlic salt

PREPARATION:

Melt the butter in a large frying pan or wok over medium-high heat. Add the dried shrimp and start frying. When the butter is starting to brown, add the sprouts. Toss them once or twice and turn off the heat. Sprinkle with garlic salt and remove from the pan. It may seem that the sprouts aren't fully cooked, but the residual heat will finish cooking them. If you leave them too long, they will become watery.

Serve immediately. Arnold likes to eat this dish with mayonnaise. Weight watchers may want to skip the extra fat and calories.

Spicy Thai Tofu Poke

Ty Katibah and Lisa Johnston opened the Natural Pacific Tofu Company in 1987. They started out in Hilo but eventually moved to the Shipman Industrial Park in Kea'au. There they make their tofu in small batches, using the finest organic soybeans and coagulating the soymilk with natural nigari, derived from seawater. They are the only tofu manufacturer in the state of Hawai'i with an Organic Processing and Handling Certification from the Hawai'i Organic Farmers Association. You can find Natural Pacific Tofu at most of our Big Island natural foods stores and at all of the KTA Super Stores.

Ty and Lisa make the usual plain tofu, as well as tofu in flavors like ginger-curry, teriyaki, and paniolo barbecue. Here's a recipe that they created to showcase the subtle but delicious taste of their plain tofu. This spicy Thai tofu poke makes a refreshing entrée on a hot day.

INGREDIENTS:
1 Family Bag (48 ounces) Natural Pacific firm tofu
1 cup chopped cilantro leaves
½ cup chopped green onions
¼ cup peeled and minced fresh ginger
¼ cup minced fresh garlic
2 tablespoons crushed red chilies (or to taste)
3 tablespoons sweet paprika
¼ cup toasted sesame seeds
⅓ cup canola oil
2 tablespoons sesame oil
¼ cup rice vinegar
½ cup soy sauce

PREPARATION:

Cut the tofu into 1-inch cubes and let it drain for 15 minutes in a colander.

Chop the cilantro, green onions, ginger, garlic, and chilies and put them into a large bowl. Add the paprika, sesame seeds, oils, vinegar, and soy sauce and mix thoroughly.

Add the drained tofu cubes to the bowl and mix gently, being careful not to break up the tofu.

Roasted Stuffed Tomatoes with Puna Goat Cheese
SERVES 4

Puna Goat Cheese is also known as Lava Rocks Farm; it's located in Hawaiian Acres, in Kurtistown. The small company sells its delicious cheeses to KTA, Island Naturals, and local farmers' markets on the east side of the Big Island. Lava's Stacey and Steve Sayre produce an assortment of cheeses: goat cheese with herbs in olive oil, chevre in various flavors, ricotta, and mozzarella.

Chef Piet Wigmans of Hilo Hawaiian Hotel has created several recipes to showcase their products. Here's one: roasted Big Island tomatoes filled with Puna Goat Cheese.

INGREDIENTS:
4 Big Island vine-ripened tomatoes
4 ounces Puna Goat Cheese
1 tablespoon finely chopped fresh basil
1 tablespoon finely chopped Italian parsley
½ tablespoon freshly-ground black pepper
1 tablespoon freshly-squeezed lemon juice (1 lemon will give this much, and more)
1 tablespoon extra-virgin olive oil
1 cup micro-greens or mesclun mix

PREPARATION:
Preheat your oven to 350°F.

Fire roast the tomatoes. (See page 44 for directions.) Peel the tomato skins. Cut off the top ½-inch of each tomato and save it; this will form a cap for the stuffed tomato. Remove the seeds and membranes inside the tomatoes with a serrated spoon.

Chop the herbs. Mix the goat cheese with the basil, parsley, and pepper. Fill the center of each tomato with ¼ of the goat cheese mixture and put on the cap. Bake in the 350°F oven for 5 minutes.

Mix the lemon juice and olive oil; this makes a simple but effective dressing. Pour this over the micro greens or mesclun mix and toss.

PRESENTATION:

Divide the greens between 4 salad plates. Place a warm stuffed tomato on each plate.

Chef Piet likes to serve this as a side dish with grilled steak.

Hilo's Fish Tempura and Kim Chee Salad
SERVES 6

There are several fish cake manufacturers in Honolulu, but only one in Hilo: Amano Fish Cake, Inc. It's great to have a source for fresh, local fish cake. I love their kamaboko and fish tempura. Hiloans in exile feel that way too; they often buy Amano products to take back as omiyage. KTA Super Stores sells fish cakes already packed in boxes, ready to carry on the plane.

The business is no longer run by Mr. Amano; he sold it in 1992. The new owners, Hiroshi and Naoe Matsubara, are experienced kamaboko and tempura manufacturers. They both come from Kanagawa, Japan, a town famous for its fish cakes. The couple ran a fish cake factory in Los Angeles before settling in Hilo and buying Amano's. They also bought the Hilo Seafood Kitchen and Big Island Tempura, expanding their product line and gaining economies of scale. Best of all, they've maintained that great Amano quality.

I like to make a quick-and-easy fish cake salad with kim chee and cucumber.

INGREDIENTS:
2 (8 ounce) packages fish cakes
1 (10 ounce) jar kim chee
2 Japanese cucumbers, washed, seeds removed
3 tablespoons rice vinegar
2 tablespoons sesame seeds

PREPARATION:
Slice the fish cakes and kim chee into ⅛-inch wide strips. Cut the cucumbers into thin 1/16-inch slices, crosswise. Mix all ingredients and chill for 15 minutes.

SMALL BUSINESSES

Mr. Ed's Sweet Dough
MAKES ONE 9 x 5½ INCH LOAF OR 12 ROLLS, BUNS, MANAPUA, OR ANPAN

The town of Honomū has boasted a bake shop for decades. First there was a shop selling manju; in 1945, Hideo Ishigo took over the location and re-opened as Ishigo Bakery. In 2000, Mr. Ed's Bakery succeeded Ishigo's Bakery. Mr. Ed serves manapua, anpan, turn-overs, cinnamon rolls, bear claws, cream buns, long johns, dinner rolls, and close to thirty different types of cookies. The store also sells jams and jellies.

Mr. Ed still uses Ishigo's old diesel oven, made by Century Machine Company of Cincinnati. The maker is no longer in business, so Mr. Ed has to search for spare parts online.

Here is Mr. Ed's basic recipe for sweet bread. This is the dough that he uses for most of his rolls, pastries, and hot dog and hamburger buns.

INGREDIENTS:

3½ cups bread flour
1 package active dry yeast (2¼ teaspoons)
¼ cup sugar
2 teaspoons salt
5 tablespoons powdered milk
¼ cup (½ stick or 2 ounces) butter
3 large eggs
½ cup water

PREPARATION:

Knead all ingredients together in an electric mixer with a dough hook attachment. The finished dough should be very smooth and flexible, and pull away from the side of the bowl; this should take about 8 to 10 minutes.

If planning to bake a loaf, form the dough into a loaf and put it in a lightly-oiled loaf pan. If making rolls, buns, or pastries, shape as appropriate on a lightly-oiled baking sheet. Let rise in a warm place for 1½ hours or until the loaf or buns have doubled in size. When the bread has almost finished rising, turn on your oven and preheat to 325°F.

Bake 20 to 25 minutes for rolls or 40 to 45 minutes for a loaf. The rolls or bread should be golden brown. Ideally, you should let the bread cool completely before cutting it; this allows the residual heat in the bread to finish cooking it. If you can't wait until it's cool, at least wait for 30 minutes or so.

Family Favorites

I just love collecting old family recipes. They're usually 'ono, and they often come with fascinating stories. Here are a few of my favorites.

Wiki Wiki Fruit Chutney
MAKES 3 CUPS

Conard Eyre, Volcano resident and owner of Green Goose Gourmet, likes to cook with Big Island fruits in season. What to do when nothing is in season? Use dried fruit!

This chutney is great with the turkey in a KTA paper bag (recipe on page 15).

Note that some people are allergic to the sulfite spray used on the dried fruits. If someone in your family suffers from this allergy, you can often buy dried fruit without sulfites at health food stores.

INGREDIENTS:
- 1 cup dried cranberries
- 1 cup dried mango
- 1 cup dried apricots
- Zest from 1 lemon
- 2 cups fresh lilikoi juice OR passion fruit juice from frozen concentrate
- 1 tablespoon red pepper flakes
- 1 teaspoon salt

PREPARATION:

Pour juice into a saucepan; add the rest of the ingredients and bring to a boil. Turn to low, and simmer for 15 to 20 minutes, or until the fruit is soft and the liquid has been absorbed. Stir frequently or the chutney may burn. When the chutney is cooked, remove it from the heat and let it sit until it reaches room temperature.

Place the chutney in a food processor and pulse only until the mixture is chunky. Do not purée. Taste to check the seasoning and correct if necessary.

Store in glass container in the refrigerator. The chutney should keep for at least 3 months.

Alan's Furikake Salmon Patties with Furikake-Wasabi Mayonnaise
SERVES 4 TO 6

Alan Fujimoto comes from a family of dentists. He became a dentist in his turn ... but if he were to take up another career, I bet he could be a top chef! He loves to cook. He cooks for his wife Phyllis and likes to host dinner parties for friends. Phyllis tells me she can barely boil water and feels so lucky to have married a such a great chef.

Here's a fancy recipe that Alan thinks nothing of making into an everyday meal. The rest of us may want to cook this delicious fish dish for special occasions.

Alan says, "You may not use all of furikake-wasabi mayonnaise. You can use any leftovers as a marinade for chicken strips. Let them marinate overnight, coat then with any leftover panko, bake at 350°F, and serve over finely shredded raw cabbage sprinkled with leftover furikake."

INGREDIENTS:
2 pounds salmon, with skin
2 cups coarse panko
1 tablespoon nori komi furikake
1½ tablespoons mayonnaise
Vegetable oil for frying

For the furikake wasabi mayonnaise:
1 cup mayonnaise
1 teaspoon prepared wasabi paste
2 tablespoons nori komi furikake
1½ tablespoons honey
⅛ teaspoon yuzu or lemon juice
⅛ teaspoon mirin

For the vegetable side dish:
1 medium carrot
1 medium zucchini
2 cups soybean sprouts
Prepared bottled ponzu sauce

PREPARATION:

To prepare the furikake salmon patties: carefully remove skin from salmon and reserve for garnish. Remove all pin bones and dark colored flesh from the salmon and discard. Slice salmon into small cubes and place into a medium bowl.

Add 2 tablespoons furikake, ¼ cup panko, and 1½ tablespoons mayonnaise to the salmon cubes. Gently toss to mix and form into 8-one inch thick patties. Place

(recipe continued on page 126)

the remaining panko into a shallow dish and coat each patty evenly. Place coated patties on a baking sheet lined with waxed paper. Chill, covered with plastic wrap for at least one hour or overnight.

Heat vegetable oil in a large frying pan and fry the salmon patties. Fry 3 or 4 at a time; do not crowd pan. Cook until golden-crisp on the outside, about a minute or two per side. Drain over wire rack with paper towels just touching the underside of the rack to wick away any excess oil.

To prepare salmon skin: Place the reserved salmon skin, skin side down on a lightly oiled cold non-stick pan. Turn on heat to low and cook skin slowly until it is crispy. Turn over and crisp the other side. Drain well on paper towels and slice into strips.

To prepare furikake-wasabi mayonnaise: Mix all ingredients.

For the vegetables: Slice carrots and green portions of zucchini into thin slices and then into julienne match sticks. Mix with soybean sprouts. Keep chilled and lightly toss with drizzle of prepared ponzu sauce before plating.

PRESENTATION:

Place the julienned raw vegetables on the plate with salmon patties. Place sliced crispy salmon skin on top and serve furikake-wasabi mayonnaise around the side of the plate. Serve with hot sticky rice.

Bea Isemoto's Lime Party Salad
SERVES 8

Isemoto Contracting is a well-known family firm that has been operating on the Big Island since the 1940s. Contractor Larry Isemoto and his wife Bea frequently enjoy this 1960s-style gelatin dessert. This isn't the kind of food that's fashionable now, but I've noticed that it disappears quickly whenever Bea serves it or brings it to a potluck. Give this recipe a try and you'll see why people come back for seconds.

INGREDIENTS:
16 large marshmallows
1 cup milk
1 (3 ounce) package lime flavored gelatin
6 ounces cream cheese, softened
1 (15½ ounce) can crushed pineapple with juice
1 cup whipped cream
⅔ cup mayonnaise (or less—Bea starts with ⅓ cup and adds more to taste)
½ cup chopped walnuts or pecans

Melt the marshmallows in the milk on top of double boiler over medium-high hea. Stir until the marshmallows have melted. Place the lime gelatin in a bowl and pour the hot milk-marshmallow mixture over the gelatin; stir till dissolved. Stir in the cream cheese and the crushed pineapple with juice. Cool. Blend in the whipped cream, mayonnaise, and nuts. Pour the mixture into a salad mold and place it in the refrigerator to set.

Aunty Helen Choy's Kochujahng Sauce
MAKES 2 CUPS

If you've eaten any Korean food at all, you've probably eaten some kochujahng (also spelled kochujang and gochujang). It's the spicy red paste with an incendiary wallop.

Old-time Korean cooks made their own kochujahng, out of hot chilies, glutinous rice, and fermented soybeans. They stored the paste in large earthenware jars and let it age in the sun, out in the backyard. Nowadays most people buy commercial kochujahng at the supermarket.

Millicent Kim's mom, Helen Choy, was a wonderful cook. We knew her as Aunty Helen. She made the most wonderful sauce from kochujahng, garlic, green onion, sugar, and vinegar. I like it with bi bim bahp, that delicious one-bowl meal.

If you have a favorite brand of kochujahng, you can use that. Aunty Helen liked the ASSI brand.

INGREDIENTS:
  1 cup kochujahng
  2 tablespoons minced garlic
  2 tablespoons chopped green onion
  ½ cup sugar
  1 cup white vinegar

PREPARATION:

Mix all ingredients together. Use as a condiment when eating bi bim bahp, haw bim bahp, and other rice bowl dishes.

Shoyu Lemon Squid
SERVES 4

The first privately owned hospital on the Big Island opened in Honoka'a in 1907. Others opened later. Some were large, like Matayoshi Hospital; others were just a few rooms, supervised by one doctor. Some of the little hospitals were Mitamura, Yamanoha, Oto, Useu, Matsumura, and Kasamoto Hospital. Most of these hospitals had closed by the 1960s.

I grew up in a house at the back of Kasamoto Hospital, where my mother worked. The doctor who ran the hospital, Doctor Sadaichi Kasamoto, and his wife Chiyo were like family to us.

Mrs. Kasamoto was a hard-working housewife and a great cook. Here is one of the recipes I remember from my childhood. Whenever I make it, I think of her.

Doctor Kasamoto liked his lemon squid with lots of hot sauce and aji-no-moto. I have left the aji-no-moto out of the recipe, as many people will not eat it, but you can add ½ teaspoon or so if you wish. You can also make the dish as hot or as bland as you like.

INGREDIENTS:
  1 (3 pound) box whole squid, thawed
  1 cup soy sauce
  5 tablespoons lemon juice (juice of 2 average lemons)
  ¼ cup sesame oil
  1 tablespoon toasted sesame seeds
  2 small onion, sliced thin
  1 teaspoon Sriracha sauce, chili-pepper water (see page 43), or other hot sauce (or to taste)

PREPARATION:

To clean the squid (if it isn't already cleaned): The squid has an external body, or mantle, which looks like a long cone with wings. Inside the cone is the internal body: the stomach, reproductive organs, ink sac, and poking out the end of the cone, the eyes, beak, and tentacles. You want to pull the internal body OUT of the mantle. You do this by grabbing the head of the squid and pulling gently, twisting if necessary.

If you don't care about keeping the mantle intact (necessary only if you're going to cut it into rings) you can insert a sharp knife into the gap between the mantle and the internal body and cut upwards, opening the squid with one long slice. Spread the mantle flat and pull out the internal body.

Now you have two pieces: the mantle and the internal body.

The mantle is stiffened by a cartilage spine called the quill. Feel for the quill and pull it out. It's inedible. The rest of the mantle is edible.

The internal body takes more processing. Cut between the eyes and the part of the internal body that was inside the mantle. Throw this part out; you won't be eating the viscera. You should be left with a head with eyes, beak, and tentacles. You can slice the head open, lengthwise, and push out the beak and the eyes. The rest of the head is edible.

Wash the cleaned squid under cold running water, inside and out. You must remove any sand, dirt, ink, and remaining tissues.

To cook the squid: Boil 2 quarts of water in a large pot. Put the cleaned squids into the boiling water and stir, so that they will cook evenly. As soon as they start to curl, remove them from the pot and drain them in a colander. Shake them to remove excess water but do not rinse them with cold water. Allow them to cool in the colander.

Juice the lemons and cut the onions. Mix the soy sauce, lemon juice, sesame oil, and onions. Slice the cooled squid into ½-inch strips or chunks. Mix the soy-lemon marinade and squid. Cover and refrigerate for 24 hours before serving.

Mrs. Ohata's Stuffed Pumpkin
SERVES 6

Harold and Yoshie Ohata moved from Honolulu to Hilo when they retired. They now live across the street from their daughter, Wendy Correa, and her family. (Wendy, by the way, was once a classmate of President Obama's at Punahou. That has nothing to do with the recipe, but it makes me feel closer to our first president from Hawai'i.)

Harold shared this recipe with me; it was one of his mother's specialties. It looks spectacular, tastes great, but isn't all that difficult to make.

INGREDIENTS:

    1 (2 pound) pumpkin (kabocha, Cinderella, or other sweet pumpkin)
    ¾ pound lean ground pork
    4 shiitake mushrooms
    ¼ cup diced carrots (⅛-inch dice)
    ¼ cup green peas
    2 teaspoons mirin or whiskey
    4 dashes Worcestershire sauce
    ½ teaspoon salt or to taste
    ¼ teaspoon white pepper or to taste
    One slice bread

PREPARATION:

Cut off the top of the pumpkin as you would if you were making a jack-o-lantern, and discard the "lid." Scoop out and discard the seeds and the stringy pulp. Wash the outside of the pumpkin with a brush and wipe dry. Salt the inside and outside of the pumpkin; this draws some of the water out of the pumpkin. You will wipe off the salt later.

Soak the shiitake mushrooms in ½ cup warm water for 15 minutes to soften. Remove the stem and cut the cap into ⅛-inch dice. Peel and dice the carrot. Thaw the green peas.

Now is a good time to preheat the oven to 350°F.

Heat a large frying pan or Dutch oven over medium-high heat. Cook and crumble the ground pork. Turn the heat down to medium and add the diced mushrooms and carrots, the thawed peas, and the water in which you soaked the shiitake. Add the mirin or whiskey and the Worcestershire sauce; season with salt and white pepper. Cut bread into ½-inch cubes and add to pork and vegetables.

Some of the water from the salted pumpkin may have drained into the bottom. Empty the pumpkin and wipe it dry. Add the filling. Place the filled pumpkin in a baking pan. Bake it in the preheated 350 degree oven for 1½ hours. Test the pumpkin with a toothpick to see if it is done; the toothpick should penetrate easily.

PRESENTATION:

You can slice this like a pie, or scoop out servings of filling and baked pumpkin meat.

Pasteles
MAKES 20 PASTELES

In August of 1899, the Caribbean island of Puerto Rico was swept by two hurricanes. The storms were followed by twenty-eight days of rain. Crops, including commercially grown sugar cane, were wiped out. Many Puerto Ricans were left homeless, without food or work. When labor recruiters from Hawaiian sugar plantations called for workers, many signed up. In December 1900, the first fifty-six Puerto Ricans arrived in Hawai'i. The second group came in January 1901 and settled on the Big Island, in Kohala, Hāmākua and O'okala.

More than a hundred years later, Puerto Rican culture and Puerto Rican cuisine are still thriving on the Big Island. All of us here have learned to love gandule rice (called honto rice here), pasteles, and ajilimojili (garlic and pepper sauce).

Pasteles are a Christmas favorite. It's a holiday tradition in many families to work together to make huge batches of pasteles, assembly line-style. This recipe has been downsized. It comes to us courtesy of Jason Morton, executive chef at Hilo Yacht Club. When his Puerto Rican grandmother gave him a cookbook, she wrote in it, "Cook with your heart and soul; just add my touch and it will be all good." She must have passed on her touch, because I love Jason's food—his pasteles in particular.

INGREDIENTS:

1½ pounds pork butt, cut into ½-inch chunks
1 cup achiote oil (recipe follows)
½ cup diced onion (⅛-inch dice)
2 cloves garlic, minced
3 stalks green onions, finely chopped (⅛-inch pieces)
½ cup chopped cilantro (¼-inch shreds)
4 Hawaiian chili peppers, seeded and minced
1 (8 ounce) tomato sauce
1 (8 ounce) can pitted olives, drained and cut in half

(recipe continued on page 132)

1 teaspoon dried oregano leaves
2 teaspoons salt
20 medium size green bananas
40 ti leaves
String

PREPARATION:

To prepare the achiote oil: In a pot, heat 2 cups oil over medium heat. Add 1 (2 ounce) package of dried achiote or annatto seeds. Simmer the seeds and oil for about 25 minutes. Drain the oil through a sieve or cheesecloth to filter the seeds out of the oil. Discard the used seeds. This recipe should make about 1½ cups achiote oil. Let the oil cool before you measure it out for the rice. Remember: achiote stains. Be careful.

To make the filling: Cut up the pork; chop the onion, garlic, green onions, cilantro, and chili peppers. Heat 3 tablespoons of the achiote oil in a large saucepan over medium-high heat and brown the pork pieces in the oil. Add the chopped onion, garlic, green onions, cilantro, and the dried oregano. Cover and simmer for 10 minutes. Stir in the tomato sauce, olives, minced chili peppers, and salt. Cook over low heat for 1 hour.

To make the dough: Soak the green bananas in hot water for 10 minutes. Peel bananas and grate finely in a blender, add a little achiote oil to thin it out.

To make the pasteles:

1. Lay out 2 ti leaves, ribs removed, side by side.

2. Put the banana dough in the center of the ti leaves and spread it out with a spatula to make a 2 x 4 inch rectangle about ¼-inch thick. Spread the filling over the banana dough to cover, leaving ¼-inch border around the dough uncovered.

3. Pick up the two sides of the ti leaves, fold over.

4. With one hand, feel where the filling ends at the stem end of the leaves and fold over to seal.

5. Stand the pastele up so the filling falls down and fills any gap. Fold the other end down to seal.

6. Turn the entire packet over.

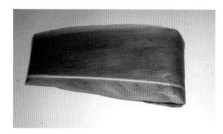

7. Cut 4 feet of kitchen twine and bring the two ends together to make a U-shape. Place on the counter and put the pastele in the middle of the twine (U-shape at the top).

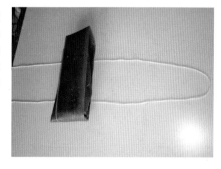

8. Lift the open ends of the twine up and pull through the top loop of the U-shape. Tighten.

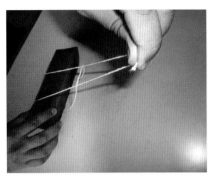

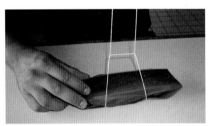

9. Then pull the ends in opposite directions, so that they are stretched cross the length of the pastele.

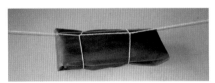

10. Turn the pastele over and tie the twine into a knot in the center of the pastele to secure.

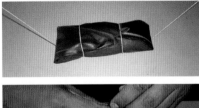

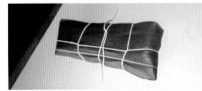

To cook the pasteles: Fill a large pot with water and add several tablespoons of salt. Bring the water to a boil. Add the tied pasteles and boil for 1 hour.

Greenwell Family Favorite Salad Dressing
MAKES ¾ CUP

There have been Greenwells in Kona since 1850, when Henry Nicholas Greenwell emigrated from England and settled on the Kona coast. He lived there for forty years: farming, ranching, growing coffee. Many descendents of Henry and his wife Elizabeth still live on the Kona coast. When the family gets together, this salad dressing will probably appear on the table. I don't think it goes back to 1850, but it is certainly good.

INGREDIENTS:

⅔ cup olive oil
¼ cup cider vinegar
2 tablespoons grated onion
2 tablespoons sugar
½ teaspoon celery salt
½ teaspoon Dijon mustard
½ teaspoon paprika
½ teaspoon salt
½ teaspoon black pepper

PREPARATION:
Grate the onion and mix all the ingredients. Whisk to emulsify.

PRESENTATION:
Serve with salad greens and perhaps some avocado, sliced mushrooms, orange sections, or bacon bits. Just not all of them at once!

Hilo-Style Potato and Macaroni Salad
SERVES 12

This is potato and macaroni salad as served by Penny Vrendenburg. She received this recipe from her mother-in-law, Edna Kelii, who was a well-known Hilo hostess and often threw parties with this Hilo-Style Potato and Macaroni Salad. It doesn't have the usual pickles, mustard, or added sugar. Carrots and peas give just a hint of sweetness. Celery, sweet onion, olives, and kamaboko add complex flavors. Penny likes to use Best Foods mayonnaise, but you can use your favorite brand—or make your own, if you like.

You'll be cooking several batches of ingredients and doing lots of chopping. Make this on a day when you aren't in a rush and can enjoy doing things one at a time, methodically and calmly. Meditation in the kitchen!

INGREDIENTS:
   3 medium size red potatoes (about 1 pound)
   5 hard-boiled eggs (large)
   12 ounces spaghetti OR 1½ cups regular small elbow macaroni
   1 cup frozen peas (omit - David doesn't like)
   2 celery stalks
   1 medium-size carrot
   ½ cup finely-chopped sweet onion (about ¼ of a medium onion)
   ½ cup finely-chopped parsley
   ½ cup sliced or chopped ripe olives
   1 (6 ounce) pink and white kamaboko (fishcake) OR
      1 (6 ounce) can tuna
   1 quart mayonnaise (more if the salad seems too dry)
   ½ teaspoon garlic powder
   Salt and pepper to taste

PREPARATION:

Cut the potatoes into ½-inch cubes (leave on the skin) and drop into a pot of boiling salted water. Boil till just tender; drain and allow to cool.

Hard-boil the eggs. If you plunge them into ice water after taking them out of the hot water, they will be easier to peel. Let them cool. Peel and grate them with a kitchen grater, coarse side. Do not chop them.

If using spaghetti, break it into 1-inch-long pieces. Cook the spaghetti or elbow macaroni in boiling salted water until al dente (just done, with still a bit of resistance when you bite into it; not soft or gummy). Drain and cool.

9/2017 8 swangers
6/2015 Mike, Vic, Brerikin's
9/2016 Megan Misuda baby shower

Cook the frozen green peas in boiling water (or steam in your microwave).

Trim and mince the celery; peel and finely grate the carrot. Peel and finely chop the sweet onion. Drain and chop the olives. If you are using kamaboko, cut it into slices and julienne slivers. If you are using tuna, drain it and break it up into flakes.

Mix all the prepared ingredients together, add the mayonnaise and garlic powder, and add salt and pepper to taste. Remember that you can add more mayonnaise if the salad seems dry.

1-8-11 mahalo party
4/11 Denise, Steve
5/11 Barley family, Vic, Mike
8/2011 - 8 swangers
10/2011 - Susan, Richard
1/2012 - meals mahalo
3/2012 friendly place
5/2012 -
Terri, Sue, Kathy

Leithead Family Scottish Shortbread

MAKES 48 (2 x 2 INCH) BARS

I still remember school days, when I could smell school lunch cooking in the cafeteria: 11 AM, still some time to wait, so hungry! My favorite menu was teriyaki fish, Spanish rice, and Scottish shortbread cookies. Those cookies were delicious!

Years later, I managed to collect the recipe for the shortbread cookies. It's a family recipe, brought over from Scotland. Vivian Leithead, cafeteria manager for Hilo High School, used it to bake my favorite school dessert. Her children, Leslie, Scott, and Bobbie Jean, shared the family recipe with me. It's amazingly simple for such a great cookie.

INGREDIENTS:
- 1 pound (4 sticks) butter
- 1 teaspoon vanilla extract
- 5 cups flour
- 1⅓ cups sugar

PREPARATION:

Preheat oven to 225°F.

Cream butter, add vanilla, mix well, then add sugar. Beat until creamy. Add flour, one cup at a time. Mix thoroughly.

Press the dough into an ungreased 12 x 17 inch baking pan with raised edges (this is what chefs call a half-sheet pan). Even out the dough and pat down so that the top is smooth. Using a fork, prick small holes all over the dough. This will help keep it flat as it bakes. Press fork around the edges to make a imprint. Bake in a 225°F oven for 1½ to 2 hours, or until the top is a light tan color.

While the cookies are still warm, use a plastic knife to cut them into 2 x 2 inch bars. Place on a wire rack and allow to cool completely before storing in airtight container or cookie jar.

Black Bean and Tortilla Bake
SERVES 6

I've known Ted and Sylvia Dixon ever since my husband retired and Ted took over as publisher of the Hawai'i Tribune Herald. *It's low fat, nutritious, easy to make, and can often be made with food that you already have in the house—no special shopping trip necessary. Oh, and it's delicious, too.*

INGREDIENTS:
1 garlic clove, minced
½ cup onion, chopped into ¼-inch dice
1 cup tomato, chopped into ¼-inch dice OR 1 cup red salsa
½ cup green onion, sliced
1 tablespoon cilantro, chopped
1 teaspoon chili powder
2 teaspoons cumin powder
1 (8 ounce) can tomato sauce
1 (16 ounce) can black beans, rinsed and drained
1 cup corn
½ teaspoon salt
1 teaspoon black pepper
12 soft whole wheat tortillas or regular tortillas
8 ounces low-fat cheddar cheese, shredded, reserving 2 tablespoons,
    OR 8 ounces regular cheddar cheese
Low-fat cooking spray for sautéing

PREPARATION:

Preheat oven to 350°F. Cut up the garlic, onion, tomato, green onion, and cilantro per the instructions in the ingredient list.

Spray a large frying pan with cooking spray. Add garlic, onions, tomato or salsa, green onion, cumin and chili powder. Cook on medium heat until the chopped onions are tender. Add tomato sauce and cook 5 minutes more. Stir in beans, salt and pepper, and cilantro. Turn off the heat.

Measure out the 2 tablespoons of grated cheese you will use for the topping and set it aside.

Spray an 8 x 8 inch baking pan with cooking spray (or use oil if you are not concerned with fat). Put 2 tortillas on the bottom of the pan. Sprinkle the tortillas with half the grated cheese (minus, of course, the 2 tablespoons), and half of the bean mixture. Lay down another 2 tortillas. Add the other half of the cheese and bean mixture. Lay down another 2 tortillas. Sprinkle the 2 tablespoons reserved cheese over the top.

Bake 20 minutes, covered, then 10 minutes uncovered or until bubbly. Let sit for 10 minutes before cutting into individual servings.

Aileen's Easy Sweet and Sour Spareribs
SERVES 6

Here's an easy meat dish from Sid and Aileen Fuke, both born and raised in Hilo. Sid was the planning director for the county; later he opened a consulting business.

INGREDIENTS:
- 5 pounds spareribs
- 1¼ cups water
- ¼ cup soy sauce
- ½ cup cider vinegar
- 1 tablespoon oyster sauce
- 1¼ to 1½ cups sugar
- 1 (1-inch) piece of ginger, crushed
- 4 cloves garlic, crushed
- Salt and pepper to taste

FOR THE CORNSTARCH SLURRY:
- 2 tablespoons cornstarch
- 2 tablespoons cold water

PREPARATION:

Put all ingredients except the cornstarch and water in a large pot with lid. Simmer over medium heat, covered, for 1 hour. Skim off any excess oil that has floated to the top.

Mix the cornstarch and cold water in a small bowl and whisk it into the spareribs. The cooking liquid will thicken into a smooth gravy.

PRESENTATION:

Sid and Aileen suggest serving this on a bed of thinly-sliced salted daikon and carrots. Rice—don't forget the rice!

Mary Stevenson's Mango Chutney
MAKES 14 CUPS

Robert Stevenson was a third generation kamaʻāina who held important positions in government and business. He and his wife Mary entertained frequently. Their son Jack now lives in Hilo, where he runs a vacation rental with his wife Jane.

Jack inherited his mother's neatly typed recipe cards. They remind him of his family's busy social life and the food that they served: old-fashioned now, but super chic in the 1960s and 1970s. Here's Mary Stevenson's mango chutney recipe; she liked to serve it with shrimp or chicken curry.

I'm sure you know that there are many mango varieties. Fruit from one tree will be sweet and delicious; another tree produces stringy mangoes that taste of turpentine and fall to the ground unwanted. How well this recipe turns out depends to a large extent on the mangoes you use. Choose well. (Farmers' Markets often have great green mangoes.)

If you like, you can soak the mango chunks overnight in a brine made with Hawaiian salt. Drain and rinse the next day, before adding to the chutney. I think this gives extra flavor to the chutney. Many people skip this step. It's up to you.

I also like to grind up the garlic, ginger, and chili peppers in my blender or food processor. Some people prefer them minced. Again, it's up to you.

INGREDIENTS:
14 cups green mangoes, sliced (approximately 13 large mangoes)
6 small or 3 large round onions, chopped
⅔ cup ginger, peeled and finely-chopped
8 small Hawaiian chili peppers, seeded and minced
8 cloves garlic, peeled and put through a garlic press
1 to 2 tablespoons orange or lemon rind, grated (optional)
3 cups walnuts, chopped (optional)
2 cups raisins (optional)
1 cup currants
7 cups white sugar
5 cups brown sugar, packed
3 cups white distilled vinegar
1 tablespoon ground cloves
1 tablespoon ground cinnamon
1 tablespoon ground allspice
1 tablespoon ground nutmeg
Salt to taste

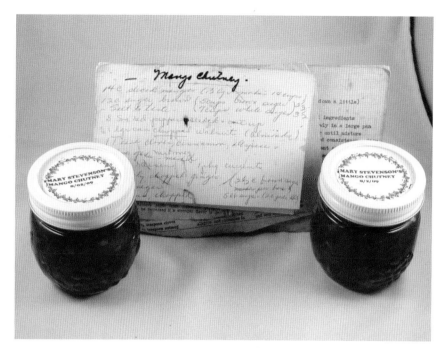

PREPARATION:

Peel and cut up the mangoes. Brine overnight if desired; drain before cooking.

Prepare the onions, ginger, chili peppers, garlic, orange and lemon rind (if using), and walnuts (if using) per the instructions in the ingredients list.

Boil the white and brown sugars, vinegar, cloves, cinnamon, allspice, nutmeg, salt in a large pot. Add the onions, ginger, garlic, chili peppers, and currants. If walnuts, raisins, and lemon or orange rind are to be used, add them now. Cook about 5 minutes. Add mangoes and cook for another 1½ hours or until mangoes are thoroughly cooked and tender rather than hard.

Sterilize canning jars and lids per the instructions on page 50. Fill the jars with the mango chutney and seal. If you are a careful canner, the jars of chutney will keep in your pantry for years.

Chicken Spaghetti
SERVES 4 TO 6

Eddie Agasa of Hilo is a fearless cook, known for his willingness to throw just about anything into the pot, his casualness about measuring, and his fondness for a nice cold beer (or two) while cooking. His adventurousness sometimes ends in disaster, but in this case, Eddie's willingness to try cooking chicken in salad dressing had a very happy ending.

If Eddie sees a few odds and ends of vegetables in the refrigerator, he may chop them fine and throw them into the pan with the bell peppers. Eddie says, "Go ahead, experiment."

INGREDIENTS:
8 ounces spaghetti, cooked al dente
6 boneless skinless chicken thighs, cut into 1-inch, bite-sized pieces
1 red bell pepper, washed, seeds removed, cut into ¼-inch strips
4 ounces button mushrooms, washed and sliced (⅛-inch thick)
1½ cups shredded Parmigiano-Reggiano cheese
⅓ cup bottled Italian salad dressing (Eddie likes Bernstein's, but any Italian dressing will do)
½ cup chicken broth (you will also need some for the slurry)

For the slurry:
2 tablespoons cornstarch
¼ cup chicken broth

PREPARATION:
Cook the spaghetti, drain, and set aside.

Cut up the chicken. Prepare the bell pepper, mushrooms, and cheese per the instructions in the ingredients list. Mix cornstarch with ¼ cup of the cold chicken broth and set aside.

Pour 3 tablespoons of the salad dressing into a large frying pan over medium heat. Lightly brown the chicken pieces in the dressing. Add more dressing if needed; add dressing any time the food begins to dry out. Add the sliced mushrooms and cook another 2 minutes. Add the sliced red peppers and cook about 3 minutes. Add the cooked spaghetti and mix well. You may need more Italian dressing to keep the noodles from sticking together. Add ½ cup chicken broth and stir to mix. Add the cornstarch slurry and stir until the sauce starts to thicken. Add the cheese and lower the heat under the pan. Cook and stir until the cheese melts; this should take about 2 minutes. Serve with more cheese sprinkled on top.

Community Favorites

I collected these recipes from community leaders (our state representatives, Clifton Tsuji and Jerry Chang) and community organizations (local firefighters, West Hawai'i Mediation Center, Kona Hospital, Hilo Medical Center, Hospice of Hilo, Hilo Hongwanji Hoyukai, and Big Island Substance Abuse Council). These folks do a lot of good; they're also good cooks. Do try a few of their specialties.

Shrimp on a Stick with Two Sauces
SERVES 4 TO 6

Hawai'i Island Home for Recovery is a non-profit organization that helps those with ad-dictions or recovering from addictions. It's a safe place to live for people who are starting over and need a helping hand to stay drug-free. Staff and clients like to cook this tasty shrimp dish, adapted from a Roy Yamaguchi recipe.

INGREDIENTS:
1 pound large shrimp
¼ cup peanut oil
Salt and pepper to taste
Bamboo skewers

For the pineapple-papaya relish:
1 large papaya, seeded, peeled and diced (¼-inch dice)
1 cup finely chopped pineapple (⅛-inch dice)
1 tablespoon finely-chopped cilantro
2 tablespoons pineapple mint
2 Hawaiian hot chili peppers, seeded and minced
2 teaspoons diced red bell pepper (¼-inch dice)
1 teaspoon minced Maui sweet onion (⅛-inch bits)
2 tablespoons lime juice (takes about 1 lime)

For the wasabi cocktail sauce:
¾ cup ketchup
2 tablespoons horseradish
2 tablespoons wasabi paste (or to taste)

PREPARATION:

Marinate the shrimp in peanut oil, seasoned with salt and pepper to taste, for 1 hour.

To prepare the relish: Chop the papaya, pineapple, cilantro, mint, chilies, and red bell peppers per the instructions in the ingredients list. Squeeze the lime. Mix all ingredients and set aside.

To prepare the cocktail sauce: Mix ketchup and horseradish, add wasabi to taste.

To cook the shrimp: Soak the bamboo skewers in warm water for 15 minutes. Skewer one shrimp, tail first onto skewer. Grill for one minute on each side.

PRESENTATION:

Serve the grilled shrimp with the pineapple-papaya relish and wasabi cocktail sauce. You can pour pools of sauce on individual plates, for a restaurant-style presentation, or you can serve a platter of shrimp with bowls of sauce on the side, and let your family and guests serve themselves.

Pumpkin Crunch Pudding Cake
MAKES ONE (9 x 13 INCH) CAKE

Brenda Ho, executive director of Hospice of Hilo, is known for her luscious desserts. One of her all-time favorites is her pumpkin crunch cake. It's a delicious variation on a pudding cake made from a mix.

It uses pumpkin pie spice, which is a pre-made blend of ground cinnamon, allspice, nutmeg, ginger, mace, and cloves.

INGREDIENTS:
1 large (29 ounce) can pumpkin
1 (12 ounce) can evaporated milk
1½ cups sugar
3 large eggs, slightly beaten
2 teaspoons pumpkin pie spice
2 teaspoons ground cinnamon
1 (10.25 ounce) box yellow pudding cake mix
1 cup pecans, chopped
½ cup butter, melted

For the frosting:
1 (8 ounce) package cream cheese, softened at room temperature
2 cups frozen whipped topping
1 cup powdered sugar

PREPARATION:

To make the cake: In a large bowl, mix pumpkin, milk, sugar, eggs, pie spice, and cinnamon. Pour into a 9 x 13 inch baking pan lined with parchment paper. Sprinkle pudding cake mix over pumpkin mixture and spread chopped nuts over the cake mix. Spoon cooled melted butter over the top. Bake at 350°F for 50 to 60 minutes. It is done when a paring knife inserted into the cake comes out clean instead of coated with batter. When cool, turn over onto serving platter.

To make the frosting: Place the softened cream cheese in a large mixing bowl, slowly blend in powdered sugar, then the whipped topping. Spread over cooled cake. Chill at least one hour before serving.

9/2023 Potter, Brauer

Hawai'i Community College's Basic Rolls
MAKES 60 ROLLS

The Culinary Program at the Hawai'i Community College teaches basic culinary skills. One of them is making sweet dough, the basis for dinner rolls, char siu bau, and sweet rolls. During the Easter holiday, students use this basic dough to make hot cross buns. Chef Instructor Allan Okuda shared the program's recipe for this very easy and always dependable dough.

INGREDIENTS:

- 13 cups bread flour
- 1 cup sugar
- 3½ teaspoons salt
- 1 cup powdered milk
- 5 large eggs
- 1 cup vegetable shortening
- 3 cups water
- ½ cup instant dry yeast

PREPARATION:

Place all ingredients except the instant yeast in the large bowl of an electric mixer with a dough hook attachment. Mix for 30 seconds, stop the motor, and add the yeast. Mix until dough is smooth and elastic, about 8 to 10 minutes.

Place in a large bowl greased with shortening or oil, cover, and set in a warm place to rise. The dough will grow best at a temperature of 84° to 88°. It will grow at the usual Big Island room temperatures, but somewhat more slowly. Let the dough rise until doubled in size; this would be about 1 hour at the ideal temperature. Dough is ready when you can press your finger lightly into the dough and leave an indentation.

Flour a smooth surface. If you have a scale, divide the dough into 2 ounce rolls. If you don't, roll the dough into logs and cut the logs into 60 equal-sized pieces. Place on a baking sheet lined with parchment paper. The rolls should be spaced 2 inches apart. Set the pan of rolls a warm area for 45 minutes, or until they have doubled in size.

While the rolls are rising, preheat your oven to 375°F.

Put the pan into the preheated oven and bake for 20 minutes, until the rolls are golden brown.

Vegetarian Chili
SERVES 6

This recipe comes from Hilo Medical Center's Food and Nutrition Services, which wants you to cook healthy, inexpensive meals. One way to do that is to cook with textured vegetable (soy) protein, or TVP. Crumbled TVP has a hearty, meat-like taste and is an excellent source of protein, fiber, and vitamins. It works well in any dish that calls for cooked, crumbled hamburger. Here it replaces hamburger in a tasty, easy-to-cook chili.

This recipe calls for canned beans. If you are on a tight budget, you can buy dried beans, cook up a large pot, and freeze the cooked beans in can-sized servings. Pull out a bag of beans when it's time to cook.

INGREDIENTS:

1 onion, chopped into ¼-inch dice
1 green bell pepper, chopped into ¼-inch dice
1 carrot, chopped into ¼-inch dice
2 stalks celery, chopped into ¼-inch dice
2 cloves garlic, minced
2 tablespoons canola oil
1 (14.5 ounce) can diced tomatoes
1 (6 ounce) can tomato paste
5 cups water
2 tablespoons chili powder
¼ teaspoon ground cumin
¼ teaspoon ground paprika
1 cup textured vegetable protein or TVP
1 teaspoon sugar
Salt and pepper, to taste
1 (15 ounce) can kidney beans
1 (15 ounce) can black beans

PREPARATION:

Chop the onion, bell pepper, carrot, celery, and garlic per the instructions in the ingredients list. You don't have to make perfect dice; however, you should try to make all the pieces about the same size, so that they will all need the same amount of time to cook.

Heat the 2 tablespoons of canola oil in a large pot over medium high heat. Sauté the onion, bell pepper, carrot, celery, and garlic until softened. Add the diced tomatoes, tomato paste, and water. Mix well. Add the chili powder, cumin and paprika. Mix again. Stir in the TVP and simmer for 15 minutes. Add sugar, salt, and pepper to taste. Stir in the beans and simmer for ½ hour.

PRESENTATION:

For maximum nutrition, serve over brown rice.

Pork Guisantes
SERVES 8

Representative Clifton Tsuji is a lifelong Hiloan. He graduated from Hilo High School, and held a variety of jobs—from radio disc jockey to bank executive—before he became involved in politics. Clif, who grew up on a plantation, remembers picking young bamboo shoots after the sugar was cut down in the summer. He gave me this fusion recipe, pork guisantes with bamboo shoots.

INGREDIENTS:
2½ to 3 pounds pork butt, cut into 1 inch cubes
4 cloves garlic, minced
1 (8.5 ounce) can bamboo shoots, cut into ½-inch slices
Canola oil for sautéing
2 (8 ounce) cans tomato sauce
½ cup water
1 teaspoon salt
½ teaspoon black pepper
3 bay leaves, broken in half
1 pound frozen peas

For the garnish:
2 (4 ounce) bottles of pimentos, thinly sliced

PREPARATION:

Cut up the pork, garlic, and bamboo shoots per the instructions in the ingredients list.

Heat the oil in a large frying pan or saucepan over medium high heat. Brown the pork and minced garlic. Add the tomato sauce, water, salt, pepper, and bay leaves. Bring to a boil, then reduce the heat and simmer for 60 to 90 minutes. Add the frozen peas and the bamboo shoots; cook until they are tender.

While they are cooking, you can slice the pimentos for the garnish.

Remove the pot from the stove and garnish the guisantes with the sliced pimentos.

Tofu Pork Hash
SERVES 6

Representative Jerry Chang's family owns Pu'ueo Poi; he grew up producing, cooking, and eating lots of great food. Now he spends much of his time at the Hawai'i State Legislature and has less time for cooking—but he still loves to cook whenever he can.

He makes this recipe with ground pork, but says that it also works well with ground turkey or chicken.

INGREDIENTS:
1 (18 ounce) block Big Island firm tofu
¼ cup dried shiitake mushrooms
¼ cup water chestnuts, cut into ¼-inch cubes
½ cup bamboo shoots, chopped into 1-inch chunks
½ cup green onions, cut into thin ⅛ inch slices
1 pound Big Island local pork, ground
2 teaspoons sake
¼ teaspoon salt
4 tablespoons soy sauce
1 tablespoon sugar
3 large eggs, beaten

PREPARATION:

Cut the block of tofu horizontally to form 4 slabs. They will each be approximately ½ inch thick. Drain the slabs on paper towels.

Soak the shiitake mushrooms in hot water to soften. Remove the stems and cut the caps into strips ¼-inch wide.

Cut up the water chestnuts, bamboo shoots, and green onions according to the directions in the ingredients list. Beat the eggs in a small bowl and set aside in the refrigerator.

Brown and crumble the ground pork in a large frying pan over medium high heat. Drain off any excess oil. Add the water chestnuts, bamboo shoots, shiitake mushrooms, sake, salt, soy sauce, and sugar. Simmer until liquid is absorbed.

While the pork is cooking, preheat your oven to 350°F.

Cover the botttom of a 9 x 13 inch baking dish with the slabs of tofu. Pour the pork mixture over the tofu and sprinkle the chopped green onions on top. Pour the beaten eggs over the layers of pork and tofu.

Bake the casserole at 350°F for 20 minutes, or until the eggs are cooked.

Picadillo

Picadillo is a Latin and Caribbean version of hamburger or minced meat in a spicy sauce. You'll find variations on picadillo in Cuba, Puerto Rico, Mexico, and the Philippines. "Pica" in Spanish means "to chop;" picadillo is made with chopped meat.

This particular version comes from Janie Chandler-Edmondson, J.D., the executive director of the West Hawai'i Mediation Center. Her grandmother brought the original recipe for picadillo from Cuba, and the dish has remained a family favorite ever since.

INGREDIENTS:

- 1 large round onion, chopped coarsely into ½-inch pieces
- 5 cloves garlic, peeled and minced
- 1 large yellow bell pepper, seeded and white sections removed, then cut into ⅛-inch strips
- 1 tablespoon olive oil
- 1 pound ground beef
- 1 (6 ounce) can tomato sauce
- 1 teaspoon dried oregano
- 1 + 1 tablespoon sugar
- ½ cup canned Spanish olives, cut in halves
- 2 tablespoons olive juice from the Spanish olives
- 2 cups raisins
- 1 large bay leaf
- 2 tablespoons ketchup
- Garlic salt to taste

PREPARATION:

Cut up the onion, garlic, and bell pepper per the instructions in the ingredients list.

Heat the olive oil in a large frying pan over medium heat; add the chopped onions and garlic. Sauté for 5 minutes, till onions are translucent. Add the chopped yellow bell pepper and cook for 1 minute. Add ground beef. Sprinkle garlic salt over the beef; start with about ½ teaspoon. Careful, as garlic salt is quite strong; taste before you add any more. Cook the ground beef until it is no longer pink, stirring frequently. Drain any excess grease from the pan.

Add the tomato sauce, oregano, and 1 tablespoon sugar. Cook on medium heat for 3 to 5 minutes, stirring frequently. Add olives, olive juice, raisins, the bay leaf, and 1 tablespoon of the ketchup. Reduce heat to medium low and simmer the picadillo for about 5 minutes. Taste and adjust seasoning. You may add the additional 1 tablespoon of ketchup and 1 tablespoon of sugar at this point, if you like.

(recipe continued on page 156)

Allow the picadillo to simmer on low for a few more minutes, until the flavors have mingled to your satisfacton.

PRESENTATION:
Serve over rice; best with fried plantains on the side (see recipe on page 157).

Sadao's Baked Ham
MAKES 24 SERVINGS

Sadao Aoki is a retired educator and an active member of the Hilo Hongwanji Mission's Hilo Buddhist Friendship Society, or Hoyukai. He enjoys cooking for his club members and has catered several events at their Sangha Hall, located next to the temple on Kīlauea Avenue. His baked ham is one of the club's favorite entrées.

INGREDIENTS:
1 (20 pound) whole ham, with bone
Handful of whole cloves
1 (20 ounce) bottle prepared mustard
1 pound brown sugar
1 quart pineapple juice
1 quart orange juice

PREPARATION:
Preheat oven to 325°F.

Score ham all over, in a diamond pattern. The cuts should be about ⅛-inch to ¼-inch deep, and the lines of scoring should be 1½ to 2 inches apart. Place cloves snugly into ham where the scoring lines cross.

Squeeze the mustard all over the ham. Pat brown sugar over the mustard. Place ham on a rack in a baking pan. Pour the orange and pineapple juice into the baking pan.

Place the pan in the preheated 325°F oven. After ½ hour, baste the ham with the liquid in the baking pan. Bake for 4 hours or until a meat thermoment shows that the meat has reached a temperature of 145 degrees in the thickest part. When taking the temperature reading, be careful not to push the thermometer all the way to the bone.

Fried Plantains
SERVES 8 TO 10

INGREDIENTS:
2 to 3 green plantains (tostones)
Olive oil to fill your frying pan ¼ inch deep

For the sauce:
1 tablespoon lime juice (about ½ average lime)
2 tablespoons crushed garlic cloves

PREPARATION:

To peel the plantains: If the peels are soft enough, you can just peel the plantains as you would a ripe banana. If the peels are harder, cut off the ends of the plantains and slice the plantains into several chunks. Make three evenly-spaced lengthwise incisions in the plantain skins. Use a paring knife to peel off the chunks of skin. If there is any skin left clinging to the plantains, use the paring knife to trim it off.

Slice the peeled plantains crosswise, into pieces no more than ½-inch thick. Save the plantain peels; you can use them later.

Pour olive oil into a frying pan until it is at least ¼-inch deep. When the oil is hot, add the plantain slices. Fry till golden on each side and transfer to a plate. You may have to do this in several batches.

When the slices have cooled a little, place each slice between two chunks of skin, or two pieces of wax paper, and use the palm of your hand to smash the slices. They should flatten and widen. There may be a few cracks around the edges; that is to be expected.

Slip the flattened slices back into the pan of hot olive oil (you may need to add a little more oil) and fry on both sides until golden brown and crisp. Place on paper towels to drain.

To prepare the sauce: Peel and crush the garlic and juice the lime. Heat 3 tablespoons of olive oil in a small pan over medium heat. Add 2 tablespoons of crushed garlic. Sauté for 2 minutes. Pour the garlic-oil mixture into a small bowl and add the lime juice. Taste and add more lime juice, to taste. Serve with the fried plantains.

Mayor Billy Kenoi's Favorite Shoyu Chicken
SERVES 6-8

Mayor Billy Kenoi is a home-grown Big Island boy. Like so many of us, he loves shoyu chicken, especially the version that his wife Takako and 3 children enjoy.

INGREDIENTS:
½ cup dried shiitake mushrooms
4 (½-inch thick) slices of peeled ginger
½ cup water
1 cup shoyu
1 cup brown sugar
5 pound box chicken thighs, thawed
Sliced green onions for garnish

PREPARATION:

Soak the shiitake mushrooms in hot water to soften. Remove the stems and slice the caps into ¼-inch strips. Peel and slice the ginger.

Put the mushrooms, ginger, water, shoyu, and brown sugar in a large pot and bring to a boil. Lower the heat to medium, add the thawed chicken, and cook for about 1 hour or until the chicken is tender. Slice up some green onions and sprinkle them over the chicken before serving.

COMMUNITY FAVORITES

Restaurants of the Big Island

In the old days, the Big Island boasted many small restaurants serving local food with a minimum of pretension. We also had a few white-tablecloth restaurants serving continental cuisine. The food landscape has certainly changed! We have more white-tablecloth restaurants, many of them serving innovative fusion cuisine that combines the best dishes the world has to offer. We have retro restaurants, ethnic restaurants, health food restaurants ... and yes, still the small restaurants serving great local food.

Here are a few more delicious recipes from the folks who work day and night to broke da mout'.

Tsunami Prawns
SERVES 4

Chef Mike Lamb of Kailua-Kona's Royal Kona Resorts developed a number of tasty recipes for the Don the Beachcomber restaurant. The menu evoked the early days of the Hawaiian tourist industry and featured favorites like ribs and steak, given a bit of sass with liliko'i, mango, coconut, pineapple, papaya, and ginger.

Chef Mike also enjoys coming up with modern fusion recipes. His recipe for prawns uses local beer, Thai chili sauce, and spicy sambal paste.

I keep bags of liliko'i purée in the freezer at all times. It's so easy to make, and I use it in many dishes. If you don't have liliko'i purée on hand, you can use passion fruit juice concentrate from the supermarket. This will change the taste a little, as the juice concentrate contains sugar and homemade purée doesn't.

INGREDIENTS:
- 12 (16–20 size) large, peeled, and deveined shrimp, butterflied
- 1 tablespoon chopped shallots OR 1 tablespoon chopped sweet onion
- 1 teaspoon garlic, minced
- 1 teaspoon chopped parsley
- 2 tablespoons olive oil
- ½ cup Mehana or Kona Brewing beer
- ½ cup sweet Thai chili sauce
- ½ cup lilikoi purée OR passion fruit juice concentrate
- ¼ teaspoon sambal chili paste

PREPARATION:

To butterfly the shrimp: cut along the back of the shrimp, as if you were going to cut it in half … but don't cut all the way. Spread it open. You may need to cut a little bit more. Put the flat of a large knife over the shrimp and press down to flatten it.

Chop the shallots or onion and mince the garlic. Remove the parsley stems and chop the leaves.

Pour the olive oil into a large sauté pan over medium heat. When the oil is hot, add shallots or onion. Saute until transparent. Add the garlic and sauté until tender; do not over cook. Burnt garlic is disagreeably bitter.

Add shrimp and continue cooking until the shrimp is slightly firm and almost pink. Add the beer and turn up the heat a little, to bring the dish to simmer. Add the sweet chili sauce, lilikoi purée, and chili paste. Bring back to simmer for a

(recipe continued on page 162)

minute or two. Remove the shrimp from the pan and arrange on a serving platter. They will cool while you are cooking the sauce, but the sauce will add just enough warmth to make the shrimp pleasant eating.

Return the sauce to the heat and simmer till reduced by half. This should take about 10 minutes. The sauce should be the consistency of syrup. At the last minute, turn off the heat and add the chopped parsley to the sauce.

PRESENTATION:

Gently drizzle sauce over the shrimp. For a restaurant touch, garnish with an orchid and some whole sprigs of parsley.

Chicken Hekka
SERVES 6

Stepping into the Back to the '50s Highway Fountain in Laupāhoehoe is like going back in time. Every available space is covered with 1950s memorabilia. Some are from owners Christopher and Kendra Ignacio's collection, but most of it—almost 80 percent, estimate the Ignacios—comes from customers. Diners like the food and the atmosphere and donate items that help create that atmosphere.

The fountain menu includes dishes that most of us old-timers remember well, like chopped steak and handmade shakes. The shakes are made in a vintage shake machine from the old soda fountain days. The restaurant is also famed for its freshly baked pies.

Christopher and Kendra were happy to share their popular chicken hekka recipe. Nothing trendy or fusion about this one, just old-fashioned good eating.

INGREDIENTS:

2½ pounds chicken thighs, chopped into ½-inch pieces
½ cup dried shiitake mushrooms
1 medium round onion, sliced into ¼-inch pieces
1 (15 ounce) can bamboo shoots, sliced into ⅛-inch slices
½ medium carrot, sliced into ¼-inch pieces
1 stalk celery, sliced into ¼-inch pieces
1 stalk green onion, sliced into 1-inch pieces
1 clove garlic, minced
1 (10 ounce) can button mushrooms
Oil for sautéing
½ cup soy sauce
¾ to 1 cup sugar, to taste
2 tablespoons oyster sauce
1 (14 ounce) can chicken broth

PREPARATION:

Cut the chicken into ½-inch pieces.

Soak the shiitake mushrooms in hot water for 15 minutes to soften. Remove the stems and slice the caps into ¼-inch pieces.

Cut up the onion, bamboo shoots, carrot, celery, and green onions per the instructions in the ingredient list.

Heat a few teaspoons of oil in a large frying pan over medium high heat. Brown the cut-up chicken and garlic. Add the soy sauce and sugar. Start with ¾ cup of sugar; you can add more later if you want your chicken sweeter. Add the oyster sauce and chicken broth. Cook over medium heat for about 10 minutes, until the liquid has boiled and started to simmer.

Reduce the heat just a little and add the onion, bamboo shoots, shiitake mushrooms, button mushrooms, carrots, and celery. Cook till vegetables are just cooked but not too soft; this may take about 20 minutes. Just before serving, garnish with green onion slices.

Macadamia Nut Mahimahi
SERVES 2

Kona Inn Restaurant has been open since 1979, ever since the old Kona Inn Hotel was converted to a shopping center. The restaurant is a great place to view the sunset over the ocean, while sipping your favorite afternoon beverage.

One of their more popular dishes is their macadamia nut mahimahi.

INGREDIENTS:
   8 to 9 ounces fresh mahimahi
   ½ cup macadamia nut breading (see below)
   Egg wash (see below)
   ¼ cup clarified unsalted butter (see recipe intro on page 64)
   1 tablespoon sesame oil
   ½ cup Napa cabbage
   2 tablespoons red bell pepper, chopped
   ¼ cup chicken broth
   ⅓ cup plum sauce (see below)
   1 tablespoon chives, chopped
   1 lemon wedge

For the breading:
   ¾ cup chopped macadamia nuts
   ½ cup fine cracker meal

For the macadamia nut egg wash:
   Flour
   1 egg
   ¼ cup half-and-half

For the plum sauce:
   1 cup plum sauce
   2 tablespoons chives
   Juice from ½ lime
   Juice from ¼ orange
   Dash salt

PREPARATION:

To prepare the plum sauce: Mix all ingredients in a mixing bowl with wire whisk. Cook the sauce in a saucepan on medium heat for 2 minutes.

To prepare the egg wash: Place enough flour on a plate to coat fish. Whip egg and half-and-half in mixing bowl and put in separate pan.

(recipe continued on page 166)

To prepare the breading: Mix all ingredients and roughly chop with food processor.

To prepare the fish: Turn oven on to 400°F. Place fish in egg wash, then coat with macadamia nut breading. Place clarified butter on flat grill, add fish, cool for approximately 45 seconds on each side and finish in oven, for approximately 10 minutes.

Heat sesame oil in sauté pan. When hot, add cabbage, red bell peppers, and chicken broth and cook for approximately 2 minutes.

PRESENTATION:

Place cooked, but still crispy Napa cabbage and bell peppers on plate. Place macadamia nut mahimahi on bed of cabbage. Pour plum sauce over top of mahimahi. Sprinkle chopped chives over top of plum sauce.

Daniel Thiebaut's Crab and Corn Cakes
MAKES 12 CAKES

Daniel Thiebaut Restaurant has been serving fine food in the former Chock In Store, in Kamuela, since 1998. Chef Daniel, born and trained in France, has applied classic techniques to local produce and meats, and to some of the fusion dishes now so popular. His restaurant was named North Hawai'i's best place for Sunday Brunch in 2009 by the North Hawai'i News.

Chef Daniel shared this recipe for crab and corn cakes. The dish is a great appetizer or light meal.

If you want to buy crabs, boil them and pick out the meat. I like to use canned or frozen crabmeat. You can also find the chili garlic sauce at the supermarket; I use the Lee Kum Kee brand.

INGREDIENTS:
½ cup chopped chives
¼ cup chopped parsley
1 + 1 cups corn kernels (fresh is best, but frozen will do)
1 cup milk
¾ cup rice flour
⅔ cup cornmeal
1½ teaspoon baking powder
4 eggs
4 egg yolks
4 tablespoons melted butter, cooled
3 cups shredded crab meat

1 teaspoon salt
1 teaspoon freshly-ground pepper
1 teaspoon chili garlic sauce
Canola oil for sautéing

PREPARATION:

Chop the chives and garlic per the ingredients list and set aside.

Combine 1 cup of the corn and the 1 cup of milk in a blender. Pour the mixture into a mixing bowl. Add the flour, cornmeal, and baking powder and mix well, either with a spoon or your mixer.

Separate 4 eggs. Put the yolks in a medium-size bowl and refrigerate the whites to use later. Crack open the other 4 eggs and add to the egg yolks. Beat well.

Melt the butter in a small saucepan or in the microwave. Add the melted butter to the eggs, slowly, whisking as you add. The eggs will thicken slightly. Pour the eggs and butter mixture into the flour mixture in the mixing bowl and mix to combine.

Add the shredded crab meat, 1 cup of corn kernels, and the chopped chives and parsley to the flour and egg mixture. Add salt, pepper and chili garlic sauce. Mix lightly. You may want to do this with a spatula rather than the beater.

Heat some canola oil in a large fry pan over medium high heat. Drop spoonfuls of the crab cake mixture into the hot oil. Cook on both sides until cooked through and golden brown. You may need to do this in several batches.

Stir-Fried Ground Chicken and Eggplant
SERVES 4

The Lam family has been operating Hilo's One Plus One Café, a Vietnamese restaurant, since 2004. The restaurant is open from 10 AM to 9 PM and serves a varied menu that includes pho and my favorite, duck funn soup.

The Lams have graciously shared this recipe for stir-fried ground chicken and eggplant. It calls for sweet soy sauce, which is made with more wheat than soybeans, and has a lighter, sweeter taste than regular soy sauce. If you can't find this in the supermarket, you can probably find it at a Vietnamese or Thai grocery. You will probably find the spicy ground bean sauce there as well.

INGREDIENTS:
10 ounces ground chicken
1 pound long Oriental eggplant
2 stalks green onions for garnish
1 teaspoon minced garlic
1 + 2 tablespoons canola oil
1 teaspoon spicy (Szechuan) ground bean sauce
¾ tablespoon fish sauce
½ tablespoon sweet soy sauce
½ teaspoon sugar
2 tablespoons chicken broth

PREPARATION:

Cut the eggplant into ½-inch pieces. You may leave the skin on or peel it off, whichever you prefer. Cut up the green onions into ¼ inch pieces and mince the garlic.

Heat 1 tablespoon of the canola oil in a wok or frying pan over medium high heat. When the oil is hot, sauté the cut-up eggplant until it turns slightly brown. Remove the eggplant slices from the oil and drain on paper towels.

Add the remaining 2 tablespoons of canola oil to the wok or pan, heat, and stir fry the minced garlic and spicy ground bean sauce until they become fragrant. Add the ground chicken and stir-fry until no longer pink. Add the already-cooked eggplant, and the fish sauce, sweet soy sauce, and sugar. Stir fry until all ingredients are warm. Add the chicken broth and briefly bring to a boil before removing the pan from the heat.

PRESENTATION:
Place on a serving platter and garnish with the green onions.

Sombat's Pad Thai
SERVES 8

Sombat's Fresh Thai Cuisine is located in Hilo's Waiakea Center in Hilo. Owner Sombat Saenguthai also manufactures a wonderful pad thai sauce that is sold at many local supermarkets and at Longs Drugs.

Sombat's pad thai is a customer favorite. You can find many pad thai recipes in cookbooks or on the internet; this one is special, thanks to Sombat's sauce.

INGREDIENTS:

1 pound (21–25 size) shrimp, shelled, deveined
1 (16 ounce) package dried rice noodles, ¼ inch size
8 cloves garlic, chopped
8 stalks green onion, cut into 1-inch pieces
4 large eggs, beaten
Canola oil for stir-frying
4 cups mung bean sprouts
½ cups roasted peanuts
1 cup Sombat's Pad Thai Sauce

PREPARATION:

Shell and devein the shrimp. Soak the rice noodles in cold water for 1 hour or until they are soft and pliable. Do not drain them until just before you are going to use them. Cut up the garlic and green onion. Crack open and whisk the eggs.

Add a little canola oil to a wok or frying pan over medium high heat. After the oil is hot, stir-fry the minced garlic for a minute or so. Add the eggs and scramble the egg-garlic mixture, stirring constantly. Add the shrimp and stir-fry until the shrimp are opaque and slightly pink; this should take about 2 minutes.

Drain the noodles and add them to the pan. Stir-fry until noodles are translucent. Pour Sombat's Pad Thai Sauce over all of the ingredients in the pan and cook for 2 minutes. Add the bean sprouts, green onions, and ground peanuts and stir-fry for 1 minute. Serve piping hot.

Sansei's Shrimp Tempura Hand Roll
MAKES 8 ROLLS

Sansei is a very popular Waikoloa restaurant, and their shrimp tempura handrolls are one of their most popular dishes. Now you can make this great handroll at home!

If you don't mind cutting corners, you can buy ready-made tempura batter at the super-market. You can also make the masago mayonnaise, the unagi glaze, and the sushi-su ahead of time. If you have a counter-top deep-fryer, with a built-in thermometer and oil storage, the deep-frying should be easier. This dish is a lot of work, but with a little planning, it's doable. Try it for special family occasions and dinner parties.

INGREDIENTS:
4 cups cooked short grain rice
⅓ cup sushi-su (see below)
8 shrimp (21–25 size), peeled, deveined, and butterflied (see directions on page 161)
8 (3-Inch long) sticks cucumber, ⅛-inch wide
8 (3-inch long) pieces green onion (slice stalks in half lengthwise and cut into 3-inch strips)
1 quart canola oil for deep frying
1 cup flour
2 cups tempura batter (see below)
4 sheets nori, cut in half
1 cup radish sprouts (kaiware), 1 inch of roots cut off
½ teaspoon roastedwhite sesame seeds, or to taste

For the masago mayonnaise:
½ cup mayonnaise
5 teaspoons masago (smelt roe)
1 teaspoon garlic, chopped

For the unagi glaze:
1 cup sugar
1 cup soy sauce
1 cup water
1 cup mirin
4 cups sake
1 tablespoon dashi-no-moto

For the sushi-su:
½ cup rice vinegar
½ cup plus 1 tablespoon sugar
2 tablespoons salt
2 (2 x 2 inch) pieces dashi-kombu

(recipe continued on page 172)

For the tempura batter:
2 cups cake flour (NOT all-purpose flour)
¼ cup cornstarch
2 teaspoons baking powder
½ teaspoon baking soda
¾ cups ice water

PREPARATION:

To prepare the masago mayonnaise: Combine the mayonnaise, masago, and garlic in a small bowl. Mix well, cover, and set aside.

To prepare the unagi glaze: Combine all ingredients in a saucepan and heat over medium heat until the sauce has been reduced to 2 cups. Cover and set aside.

To prepare the sushi-su: Bring the vinegar to a boil, add the sugar, salt, and kombu, and simmer until the sugar has completely dissolved. Remove the strip of kombu. You will not need all of this sushi-su for the handrolls. The leftover su will keep in the refrigerator for several months.

To prepare the sushi rice: Cook the 4 cups of rice. Put the rice in a flat pan or, if you have one, a wooden tub for making sushi rice. Add 13 cup sushi-su to the hot rice and start to turn and mix the rice. The cooling rice should absorb the sushi-su. If you have a table fan, turn it on the rice to speed up the cooling and the absorption.

To prepare the handroll fillings: Peel, devein, and butterfly the shrimp; cut up the cucumber, green onions, and radish sprouts per the instructions in the ingredient list.

To prepare the tempura batter: Whisk together the flour, cornstarch, baking powder, and baking soda in a medium-size bowl. Add the ice-cold water. Whisk until just mixed. If there are a few lumps, that's fine; leave them. If you over-mix the batter, you will develop the gluten in the flour and the batter will be tough.

To cook the shrimp: Pour oil in a deep pan until it is 2 inches deep. Heat the oil to 325°F. A deep-frying thermometer helps.

Dip shrimp in flour and then in tempura batter. Fry until golden-brown, turning once. Drain on paper towels.

TO ASSEMBLE:

Line up all your ingredients—the just-fried shrimp, the masago mayonnaise, the unagi glaze, the cucumber and green onion, the radish sprouts, the sesame seeds, and the sheets of nori. Cut the nori in half.

Put about ⅛ of the rice on a half-sheet of nori; spread masago mayonnaise on the rice. Along one edge of the nori, put a line of radish sprouts. Lay the cucumber stick, slivers of green onion, and one shrimp tempura on top of the sprouts. Brush the shrimp with some unagi glaze and sprinkle it with white sesame seeds. Roll tightly into a cylinder or a cone shape, beginning at the end with the shrimp. Repeat until all the shrimp are rolled up.

PRESENTATION:

Serve with the remaining unagi glaze as a dip.

Sansei's Rock Shrimp Dynamite
SERVES 6

Another popular Sansei dish is their rock shrimp dynamite. Owner D. K. Kodama was willing to share this recipe too. Thanks, D. K.!

This dish uses many of the same ingredients as the shrimp tempura handroll. If you like both recipes, you might want to make extra-large batches of the masago mayonnaise and the unagi glaze.

INGREDIENTS:
  Canola oil for deep-frying
  6 (2 x 2 inch) wonton wrappers
  3 cups rock shrimp, peeled and deveined
  2 cups flour
  5 cups tempura batter (see recipe on page 172)
  4 cups mixed greens, loosely packed
  ¾ cup unagi glaze (see recipe on page 171)
  ¾ cup masago mayonnaise (see recipe on page 171)

For the garnish:
  6 tablespoons finely chopped green onions, green part only
  ½ cup white sesame seeds, toasted

PREPARATION:

Pour at least 4 inches of oil into a heavy saucepan and heat to 350°F. A deep-frying thermomenter will help here. Deep-fry the wonton wrappers, turning them with tongs so that they cook evenly. They should be golden brown and crisp. This should take about 3 minutes. Using a slotted spoon, transfer the wontons to paper towels and let them drain. Turn off the heat under the oil while you prepare the shrimp.

Toss the shrimp in the flour until they are evenly coated. Shake off the excess flour. Return the oil to 350°F. Dip a few of the shrimp in tempura batter; they should be completely coated. Transfer them to the oil and fry until golden brown, which should take about 3 to 4 minutes. Using a slotted spoon, transfer the cooked shrimp to paper towels. Repeat until you have cooked all the shrimp. If you try to cook them all at once, you will crowd the oil and the shrimp will be soggy and oily.

(recipe continued on page 176)

Put the masago mayonnaise in a bowl and add the shrimp. Gently mix until the shrimp are evenly coated.

PRESENTATION:

To serve the shrimp restaurant style, set out 6 serving plates. Put a mound of greens on each plate; top each mound with a fried wonton and ⅙ of the shrimp.

Drizzle unagi sauce over each plate and top with the chopped green onions and the sesame seeds. For a family-style presentation, arrange all the greens, wontons, and shrimp on a serving platter; drizzle with sauce and add the garnish.

Chicken Satay with Peanut Sauce
MAKES 32 SKEWERS

Sous-chef Bryceson Velez of the Mauna Lani Bay Hotel and Bungalows has worked hard to perfect his version of chicken satay.

The recipe looks long and complicated, but the only part of it that requires much work is the optional lemongrass in the peanut sauce. You may want to double the amount of sauce; it's good with so many foods: noodles, steamed vegetables, grilled meat and poultry.

INGREDIENTS:
2 pounds boneless, skinless chicken thighs
32 bamboo skewers

For the satay marinade:
1½ teaspoons ground coriander
1½ teaspoons ground cumin
1½ tablespoons curry powder
¼ teaspoon turmeric
¼ cup sugar
1½ tablespoons garlic, chopped
1½ tablespoons ginger, grated
1½ tablespoons fish sauce or Thai nam pla
1 cup coconut milk
1½ tablespoons water
¼ teaspoon kosher salt

(recipe continued on page 178)

1 to 2 teaspoons red Thai curry paste, or to taste (less if you don't want if too hot)
1 cup coconut milk
½ cup peanut butter (more if you want it thicker)
2 tablespoons chicken marinade
1 kaffir lime leaf, bruised but left whole
1 stalk lemongrass (optional)
2 tablespoons roasted peanuts, chopped, for garnish
Canola oil for sautéing

PREPARATION:

To marinate the chicken: Cut each thigh (you'll have about 8) into 4 even pieces. Chop the garlic and mix all marinade ingredients thoroughly. Place chicken pieces on skewers and dip in the marinade. Cover and leave in the refrigerator for 3 hours. Turn the chicken pieces occasionally so that they marinate evenly.

If you are using lemongrass in the peanut sauce: strip off any dried leaves and cut off the bulb. Cut across the stem at ¼ inch intervals, or closer, until you have a stack of tiny rounds. Put the rounds into a food processor and process until you have a pile of lemongrass fragments. These should soften when cooked in the sauce. You may want to taste the finished sauce to check; if the lemongrass bits are still dry and hard, you may need to strain them out.

The upper half of the stalk will probably be too dry to cook this way. You can use it in the sauce if you make a series of shallow cuts crosswise on the stalk and bend it a few times, to bruise it and release the juices. Let it simmer in the sauce and them remove it before serving.

To prepare the peanut sauce: Crush the lime leaves. Fry the leaves and the Thai curry paste in a little canola oil until they start to smell spicy and delicious. This should take only 30 seconds or so. Add the remaining ingredients and simmer for 5 minutes. Turn off heat and let the sauce steep for another 15 minutes before cooling. Remove the lime leaves and any lemongrass stalks before serving.

Grill chicken skewers over hot coals or an electric grill, 5 minutes on each side, until chicken is thoroughly cooked. Serve with peanut sauce on the side.

Green Apple Mustard
MAKES ⅔ CUP

Monettes Restaurant at the Mauna Kea Beach Resort is owned by Scott and Mark Monette. They grew up in the restaurant biz: their father operated a restaurant in Boulder, Colorado. He collects wine and Scott and Mark have been given (and serve) some of their father's amazing vintage wines.

Matthew Zubrod is the both chef and general manager at Monettes. He shared his recipe for this wonderful green apple mustard. The restaurant serves it with cheese and walnut bread. It is so tasty that I am sure you will find other uses for it.

INGREDIENTS:
- 1 shallot, peeled and minced fine, about 2 tablespoons
- 2 Granny Smith apples, peeled, cored and cubed into ½-inch pieces
- 3 tablespoons yellow mustard seeds
- 2½ tablespoons brown mustard seeds
- 2 tablespoons apple pucker liqueur
- ⅓ cup white wine
- ⅓ cup apple cider vinegar
- ¾ teaspoon salt
- ¼ teaspoon white pepper
- 4 drops green food coloring

PREPARATION:

Cut up the shallot and the apples per the instructions in the ingredient list. Feel free to cut the apples even finer than ½ inch. The smaller the pieces, the faster the apples will cook.

In a non-reactive (enamel or stainless steel) sauté pan over medium heat, toast the mustard seeds until they begin to pop; this should take about 2 to 3 minutes. Stir constantly, or they will burn. Add the chopped apple and shallot. Pour in the apple pucker liqueur and use to deglaze the pan (deglazing dissolve any cooking residues, which provide extra flavor). Cook over medium low heat until the apples are soft, about 20 minutes. Add more liqueur as needed so the apples do not burn. Remove from heat and add the wine, vinegar, salt, pepper, and food coloring. Cover and refrigerate overnight. This allows the flavors to blend.

The next day, transfer the mustard mixture to a blender and process until the mustard is well-ground. You can store this mustard in an airtight glass jar in the refrigerator for up to 2 weeks.

Burgundy-Style Rabbit Stew
SERVES 6

La Bourgogne French Cuisine, in Kailua-Kona, has been serving the regional cuisine of Burgundy for over twenty-five years. Owners Ron Gallaher and Colleen Moore shared this recipe for rabbit. It's a relatively easy dish that uses one technique that may be new to you: flambé. If you have never intentionally set your food on fire, this is your chance.

Rabbit to make this dish can be purchased at Island Gourmet, located in the Queen's Marketplace in Waikoloa.

INGREDIENTS:
- 1 rabbit, cut into pieces, disjointed
- 4 shallots, chopped
- 2 carrots, peeled and cut into 2-inch chunks
- 4 baby turnips, peeled and cut into 2-inch chunks
- ½ pound snow peas, strings removed
- ¼ cup chopped Italian flat leaf parsley
- 2 tablespoons butter
- Salt and pepper to taste
- ¼ cup brandy
- ¼ cup red wine
- 2 tablespoons flour
- 2 cups chicken broth

PREPARATION:

Start by cutting up the rabbit, shallots, carrots, and turnips, stringing the snow peas, and chopping the parsley.

Heat the butter in a heavy-bottomed pan over medium heat. Add the chopped shallots and sauté until translucent. Add the rabbit pieces and brown on all sides. Season with salt and pepper.

Increase the heat and add the brandy and red wine. Flambé the liquid. Yes, just put a match to it. If you're nervous, use one of the long matches made for barbecuing and keep the pot lid handy, to smother the flames if you feel it's necessary. The alcohol in the brandy will catch fire and burn blue. It burns down quickly. The flame sears off the alcohol content, but leaves a pleasant brandy taste.

Sprinkle the flour over the rabbit and mix well. Pour in the chicken broth, add the cut-up carrots and turnips, and cover with the pot lid. Cook over medium heat for 40 minutes, stirring occasionally.

Blanch the snow peas in boiling water for 1 minute, then cool in running cold water. You are cooking them separately so that they will stay nicely crisp.

When the rabbit is done, add the blanched snow peas and cook for another 5 minutes. Add the ¼ cup chopped parsley and serve.

Celebrations, Festivals, and Lūʻau

My husband and I go to many celebrations: for business, for community, for family. We attend sit-down dinners, buffets, food fairs, and lūʻau. Everywhere we go, we find good food. Big Islanders are great cooks! Naturally, when I taste something extra special, I make every effort to collect a recipe. Here are a few of my finds.

Purple Sweet Potato Salad
SERVES 6 TO 10

Lū'au, graduations, reunions—whenever Big Islanders get together, you're likely to find a bowl of purple sweet-potato salad. Here's an upscale version, from Eric Lelinski, executive chef at the Sheraton Keauhou Bay Resorts and Spa.

INGREDIENTS:
- 8 Hawaiian purple sweet potatoes
- 2 stalks celery
- 1 small sweet onion
- 1 medium carrot, peeled
- 1 cup mayonnaise
- ¼ cup coconut syrup
- ¼ cup shredded sweetened coconut

PREPARATION:

Boil the sweet potatoes, unpeeled, in salted water until they are tender; this should take about 15 to 20 minutes. Let them cool in the refrigerator. Peel the cooled potatoes and cut them into 1-inch cubes or chunks.

Finely chop the celery, onions, and carrots into ⅛-inch pieces.

Put the mayonnaise, chopped vegetables, and coconut syrup in a large bowl and mix. Add in potatoes and mix gently, being careful not to mash the potatoes. Store the salad, covered, in the refrigerator for 1 hour before serving. This allows the flavors to mingle. (Actually, this salad tastes even better two days later!)

While the salad is resting, toast the coconut for the topping. You can do this in the oven or in a frying pan on the stove top. The coconut won't brown as evenly in the frying pan.

For oven toasting, heat oven to 300°F. Spread the coconut in a thin layer on a baking sheet or pan with low sides. Bake for about 20 minutes, stirring every five minutes. Coconut burns easily.

To toast in a frying pan, cook coconut over medium heat, stirring frequently.

PRESENTATION:
Top the salad with the freshly-toasted coconut and serve.

Maharaja Shrimp with Pineapple Chutney

MAKES 12 SKEWERS

S. Lynn Fukuda and Sachi Ogawa were married in 1959. Fifty years later, they celebrated their golden anniversary at a special dinner for family and friends. The Sky Café, at the 'Imiloa Astronomy Center, catered a fantastic feast, ending with a wedding cake that celebrated fifty years of happiness.

Sachi planned the menu and paid particular attention to the appetizers. She is after all, the author of a local cookbook titled Pupus: Island Adaptations. *One appetizer, the shrimp, was so delicious that I just had to have the recipe.*

It looks complicated, but the chutney can be made ahead of time, and the marinade is easy. Marinate the shrimp for 1 hour and fire up the grill. It's that simple!

INGREDIENTS:

24 large shrimp (21–24 size), peeled, deveined, tails left on
12 (5-inch) bamboo skewers

For the chutney:

1 cup minced fresh pineapple
½ cup sugar
1 (6 ounce) can pineapple juice
3 tablespoons lime juice (about 1 or 2 limes; buy 2 to be safe)
¾ teaspoon chili garlic sauce (you'll find this in the Oriental section of the store)
2 teaspoons cornstarch
2 teaspoons cold water
¼ teaspoon salt

For the marinade:

½ cup plain yogurt
2 tablespoons fresh ginger, minced
2 tablespoons garlic, minced
1 tablespoon lemon juice
2 teaspoons curry powder
½ teaspoon paprika
½ teaspoon salt
1½ teaspoons sugar

For the garnish:

Fresh chopped mint
Lime juice

(recipe continued on page 186)

To prepare the chutney: Mince fresh pineapple and juice the lime or limes. Simmer pineapple, sugar, pineapple juice, 3 tablespoons lime juice, and chili garlic sauce in a saucepan over medium-high heat for 8 minutes. Stir together cornstarch and cold water, add to pineapple mixture, and simmer until thickened. Season with salt. Refrigerate until ready to serve.

To prepare the marinade: Peel and mince the ginger and garlic. Combine the yogurt, ginger, garlic, lemon juice, and seasonings in a bowl. Add shrimp, toss to coat, cover and refrigerate for 15 to 30 minutes. Do not marinate for more than 1 hour. The shrimp will get mushy.

While the shrimp is marinating, soak the bamboo skewers in water. If you don't, the skewers will burn when you grill the shrimp. Chop the mint and squeeze the lime juice for the garnish.

TO GRILL THE SHRIMP:

Thread 2 shrimp onto each bamboo skewer, scraping off excess marinade. You can either grill the shrimp over a charcoal grill, or you can use a grill pan on the kitchen stove. If grilling on the stove, spray a grill pan frying pan with nonstick spray and preheat the pan over medium heat. Add the shrimp skewers and grill until the shrimp are firm; this should take about 2 to 3 minutes per side.

PRESENTATION:

Arrange skewers on a platter, drizzle with lime juice, and sprinkle with chopped mint. Serve with the chutney.

Taro Muffins
MAKES 12 MUFFINS

I enjoyed the muffins at the Kona Village Resort so much that I begged Chef Mark Tsuchiyama for the recipe. It uses some of our fine local taro.

INGREDIENTS:
- ½ pound taro, cooked, peeled, and cut into ¼-inch dice
- 1½ cups (6 ounces) bread flour
- 1 tablespoon baking powder
- ½ cup plus 2 tablespoons (4 ounces) sugar
- ½ cup butter, softened
- ½ teaspoon salt
- 2 large eggs
- ½ cup milk
- 2 tablespoons honey
- 2 tablespoons coconut syrup
- ½ cup wheat bran

PREPARATION:

Boil the taro. Don't peel it first; the oxalic acid crystals will burn your hands. Boil, then peel and dice.

Preheat the oven to 375°F. Grease a muffin tin, or use muffin tin liners.

Sift together the flour and baking powder. Cream together the sugar, butter, and salt. Combine eggs and milk and add to the butter mixture in three increments until fully incorporated. Add honey and coconut syrup until incorporated. Then add dry ingredients until just moistened. Gently fold in the diced taro. Scoop the batter into the greased or lined muffin tins until the pukas are ¾ full.

Bake in 375°F oven for 25 minutes or until a toothpick inserted in the middle of a muffin comes out clean. Cool the muffins in the tins. Remove when cool and serve.

Ohagi

Ohagi are sweet rice balls with tasty top-pings and wrappings, often made with an (bean paste). In old Japan, they were made for the higan days, at the spring and autumn equinoxes, when families gathered to clean the family graves and make offerings. Ohagi were put out as offerings and also shared by family members. (Actually, ohagi are the autumn offerings and botamochi are the spring offerings, but everyone calls them both ohagi these days.)

For the Big Island's Japanese-American families, ohagi is festival and family gathering food. I recently had some delicious ohagi at a Takajo family gathering and managed to get the recipe. The Takajos like to get together during the summer. Last year, sixty Takajo family members came from all over the mainland and the Islands to Kurtistown, to meet their relatives. Different generations looked over old photos together, reminiscing about times gone by. Naturally, ohagi were served. The Takajos also make ohagi for Girls Day, Boys Day, and birthdays.

Perhaps I love ohagi because they remind me of good times with family.

INGREDIENTS:
1½ cups mochi rice
½ cup short-grain rice
2 cups water
1 (12 ounce) can prepared tsubushi or koshi-an (bean paste)
⅛ teaspoon salt dissolved in ½ cup water (to moisten hands)

PREPARATION:
Cook the rice in rice cooker with 2 cups water. While the rice is still hot, mash rice grains with a wooden spoon or pestle, until you have a mass with a texture like mochi (but not as uniform). Dampen your hands with the salt water and form the rice into balls about about 1½ inches in diameter.

To cover the rice balls with a layer of tsubushi or koshi-an; put the an in a micro-wave-safe dish and warm it a little in the microwave. Cook in short bursts until it is pleasantly warm. You don't want to overcook and burn it.

Lay a sheet of plastic wrap on the counter and put 1 tablespoon of the an in the middle. Spread out the an with a rubber spatula. Place a rice ball in the center of the an. Pick up the edges of the plastic wrap and ease the an around the rice ball.

Kuhio Grille's
Famous Baked Short Rib Stew
SERVES 10

Taste of the Range is an annual food fair and exposition held to celebrate the Big Island ranching industry; beef, lamb, and pork are featured. I love this fair! I can sample wonderful dishes from the island's best chefs and taste some cuts of meat that I don't ordinarily buy, such as tripe and mountain oysters.

The Kuhio Grille restaurant presented a tasty short rib stew. The chef made a point of using convenience foods like dry soup mix and canned soup, showing that an easy-to-cook dinner can be a good dinner.

INGREDIENTS:
    5 pounds Kamuela Pride thick-cut short ribs
    2 medium carrots
    2 medium round onions
    3 medium potatoes
    1 (4 ounce) package onion or mushroom dry mix soup
    3 cans (10¾ ounce) cream of mushroom soup
    1 can (10¾ ounce) tomato soup

PREPARATION:

Preheat oven to 375°F.

Cut up the ribs into bite-sized pieces. Peel and chop the vegetables (¾-inch dice or chunks). Mix all ingredients in a large bowl. Transfer into a baking dish. Bake for 3 to 4 hours, or until the meat and vegetables are tender.

Chilled Wild 'Ōhelo Berry Soup
SERVES 3 TO 4

'Ōhelo berries grow wild at higher elevations on the Big Island. These delicious fruits are related to the huckleberries of the Pacific Northwest. Like their mainland cousins, they make tasty jams, preserves, sauces, and topping for cheesecakes. They also make great pies, if you can gather enough of them.

Scientists at the University of Hawai'i's Volcano and Waimea Experimental Stations are cultivating 'ōhelo bushes in the hopes of learning how to grow them commercially. Wouldn't that be wonderful? Your neighborhood KTA would always have 'ōhelo berries on sale.

Until that day, you'll just have to pick wild berries. Here's a great recipe for a cold soup made with 'ōhelo berries, from Executive Chef George Gomes of the Mauna Kea Beach Resort, who cooks with the berries whenever he can get them.

INGREDIENTS:
1½ cups wild 'ōhelo berries
2 tablespoons lemon juice (juice of 1 average lemon)
2 tablespoons sour cream
2 tablespoons Big Island honey
2 tablespoons Grand Passion liqueur
Apple juice, as needed
Fresh mint sprigs and extra 'ōhelo berries, for garnish

PREPARATION:
Put the berries, lemon juice, and sour cream in a blender and purée until smooth. Add a little at a time of the honey and liqueur until you like the taste. If you need to thin the soup, add apple juice slowly until the soup is the consistency of thick cream.

PRESENTATION:
Serve the soup in a chilled demitasse cup or small bowl and garnish with whole 'ōhelo berries and fresh mint sprigs.

Mango Bread Pudding
MAKES ONE 9 x 13 INCH PAN OF PUDDING

Mangoes grow well in the drier parts of Kona. In 2009, we attended the First Annual Mango Festival in Keauhou, Kona. I was able to taste mango jams, butters, smoothies, salsas, shave ice, entrées, and desserts; hear informative talks; and learn about the many varieties of mango developed by our agricultural scientists. It was fascinating, and I'm looking forward to this year's festival.

Chef Cy Yamamoto of the Keauhou Beach Hotel demonstrated a mango-inspired dinner and finished with a delicious mango bread pudding. Here's the recipe.

INGREDIENTS:

  1 loaf Punalu'u Sweet Bread
  4 large mangoes, (Hayden or other large sweet mango is good)
  2 quarts heavy cream
  16 egg yolks
  2 tablespoons Hawaiian vanilla extract
  ¼ cup brandy

PREPARATION:

Preheat your oven to 350°F.

Cut the sweet bread and the mangoes into 1-inch cubes or chunks and gently mix. Spread over the bottom of a buttered 9 x 13 inch baking dish.

Slowly heat the cream in a large saucepan over medium heat; do NOT let it boil. Keep the heat low while you separate the eggs.

Put the egg yolks in a large bowl and mix or whisk until they turn a pale yellow; this should take about about 5 to 6 minutes. Add the brandy and mix or whisk for another minute.

Slowly add pour 1 cup of the warm cream to the egg mixture, mixing or whisking constantly. This will warm up the eggs, without turning them into scrambled eggs. Pour the eggs back into the remaining cream in the saucepan, stirring constantly. Add the vanilla and mix well.

Pour the egg yolk–cream mixture over the bread and mango cubes in the baking dish. Bake in the preheated 350°F oven for 45 minutes, or until a knife stuck in middle of bread pudding comes out clean.

Note: Freeze the egg whites for later use.

Squid Lūʻau
SERVES 4

When Kanoelehua Mary Ho, of the Big Island, graduated from Kamehameha Schools in 2009, the Ho family held a big graduation lūʻau at Wailoa State Park. What an affair! Clyde Ho organized and cooked, and he is one great cook. He used twenty-five pounds of lūʻau leaves (the young, tender leaves of the taro plant). One of the dishes he made was this tasty squid lūʻau. He made it for a few hundred; I've cut the recipe down, so that you can make it for a family meal.

Note that you add the squid only at the end and cook it briefly. This is one way to make sure that it's tender and tasty.

INGREDIENTS:
4 cups cooked lūʻau leaves (start with 5 pounds of raw leaves)
2 cups squid, cleaned and cut-up (start with 2 pounds of cleaned squid)
¼ cup butter
2 cups coconut mllk
Hawaiian salt, to taste

PREPARATION:

To prepare the lūʻau leaves: Cut off about ½-inch from each of the three points of the leaf tips. Cut off the stem, right next to the leaf. Peel off the large vein that runs along the center of the leaf. Put the leaves in a large pot, add water to cover and a pinch of baking soda (about 1 teaspoon), and bring to a boil. Cook for about 15 minutes. Drain. Put the leaves in the pot again, add water and baking soda again, and boil for another 15 minutes. Drain and boil for one last time. You'll probably need to cook the leaves for 45 minutes total (15 + 15 + 15). Taste the leaves at the end; if they aren't tender, cook them a little longer.

Cut the cleaned squid into ½-inch pieces.

Melt the butter in a large pot over medium heat. Stir in the cooked lūʻau leaves and cook until warm and soft. Add the coconut milk and mix well. Stir in the squid and add salt to taste. Add more coconut milk if you feel the mixture is too thick. Increase the heat slightly, bring to a boil, and immediately turn off the heat. Serve immediately.

Hilo Huli Mushroom Soup
SERVES 8 TO 10

Hilo Huli is an annual fundraiser for the Rotary Club of South Hilo. It is held on the first Sunday in May, at Coconut Island or Mokuola Island.

Chef Albert Jeyte of Kīlauea Lodge created a wonderful soup for the 5th annual Hilo Huli. He called it Hilo Huli mushroom soup.

INGREDIENTS:
- 1 cup red bell pepper, diced ⅛-inch (about 1 pepper)
- 1 cup green bell pepper, diced ⅛-inch (about 1 pepper)
- 1 cup round onions, diced ⅛-inch (about 1 onion)
- ½ pound button or white mushrooms, diced ⅛-inch
- ¾ cup garlic, finely-chopped
- ¼ cup (½ stick) butter
- 1 teaspoon dried oregano
- 1 teaspoon dried marjoram
- 1 teaspoon finely ground black pepper
- 1 teaspoon salt
- 1 cup flour
- 12 cups chicken broth
- ¼ cup plus 2 tablespoons sweet curry powder
- 12 ounces sour cream
- 1 (13.5 ounce) can coconut milk

FOR THE CORNSTARCH SLURRY:
- ½ cup cold water
- 2 tablespoons cornstarch

FOR THE GARNISH:
- ¾ ounces sweetened coconut flakes
- 1 stick butter

PREPARATION:

Cut up the bell peppers, onion, mushrooms, and garlic per the instructions in the ingredients list.

Put the butter in a large 1-gallon stockpot over low heat. When the butter is melted, add the peppers, onions, mushrooms, garlic, oregano, marjoram, black pepper, and salt. Sauté for 6 to 7 minutes , stirring occasionally, until the peppers and onions have softened.

Add the flour and stir for 4 to 5 minutes. The flour and melted butter will combine to make a golden roux, the flour-butter paste that is the basis of many sauces.

Slowly add the chicken broth, whisking constantly. The stock should thicken. The whisking prevents lumps. Turn the heat up to high and bring the sauce to a boil, continuing to whisk constantly. Turn down the heat again, whisk in the curry powder, and simmer the mixture, covered, for about 20 minutes. Occasionally remove the lid and stir.

While the soup is simmering, prepare the coconut for the garnish. Melt the 2 ounces of butter in a sauté pan over low heat. Add the coconut flakes and cook, stirring constantly, until the coconut flakes are light to dark brown.

When you are ready to serve the soup, add the sour cream and coconut milk and bring to a slow boil again. Turn down the heat and simmer an additional 5 minutes, until sour cream is incorporated into the soup. Mix the cornstarch and water to form a slurry and add to the soup, stirring constantly as the soup thickens.

PRESENTATION:

Pour the soup into soup bowls and sprinkle with toasted coconut flakes.

Rolled Prosciutto Ham Quesadilla with Green Apple Salsa
SERVES 6 TO 8

The 11th annual Taste of Hilo food fair was held in October 2009 at Hilo Hongwanji's Sangha Hall. Over thirty vendors were there to show off their delicious food. I was particularly taken with Café Pesto's ham quesadilla. Chef Casey Halpern used many local food products; the tasty result was a tribute both to his skill and to the hard work of our local farmers and food manufacturers.

INGREDIENTS:

For the quesadilla:
½ cup Hāmākua mushrooms
2 tablespoons jalapeño peppers, minced
1 clove garlic, peeled and minced
½ cup extra virgin olive oil
½ cup prosciutto ham
6 Big Island flour tortillas
½ cup smoked mozzarella or Monterey Jack cheese, shredded
¼ cup Big Island goat cheese, crumbled
Salt and pepper to taste

For the salsa:
2 medium green apples, peeled, core removed, cut into ¼-inch pieces
3 tablespoons fresh lime juice (about 2 limes)
¼ cup sweet onion, diced (¼-inch pieces)
¼ cup cilantro, chopped
¼ cup yellow bell pepper, diced (¼-inch pieces)
¼ cup red bell pepper, diced (¼-inch pieces)
2 tablespoons green onion, chopped
2 tablespoons garlic, finely minced
½ cup Hāmākua Springs cocktail tomatoes, puréed in blender
1 tablespoon hot sauce
1 tablespoon honey
Salt and pepper to taste

For the garnish:
About ½ cup sour cream, to top quesadilla

PREPARATION:

To prepare the salsa: chop vegetables per instuctions in ingredients list. Cut up the apples first. After you squeeze the limes, put the lime rinds in a bowl of ice

(recipe continued on page 198)

water and add the chopped apples. The lime will keep the apple from browning and the water will ensure that the apples are crisp. When all other ingredients have been cut, drain the apples. Mix all salsa ingredients together and adjust seasoning with salt and pepper. Cover and set aside.

TO PREPARE THE QUESADILLAS:

Clean the mushrooms and cut them into thin slices. Trim, deseed, and mince the jalapeño peppers. Peel and mince the garlic.

Heat the olive oil in a large frying pan over medium heat; fry the prosciutto until it is crisp. Drain the prosciutto on paper towels and when it has cooled, gently crumble it.

Using the same oil, fry the tortillas until brown but soft enough to roll. Unless you have a large pan, you will probably have to do this one at a time. Put the tortillas on a plate and cover with a towel, to keep warm. Add more olive oil as needed.

Add the mushrooms, jalapeño peppers, and minced garlic to the pan and cook until the mushrooms wilt. Add salt and pepper to taste.

Preheat oven to 350°F. Shred and crumble the cheeses.

Cut the tortillas in half; you will have 12 halves. Lay them out on the counter and divide the crumbled prosciutto, cooked mushrooms, and shredded cheeses evenly between the tortilla halves. Put the filling in the center and roll the tortilla halves into cones.

Place the quesadillas in a baking dish and bake at 350°F for 10 minutes.

PRESENTATION:

Top with sour cream and green apple salsa.

Coffee-Encrusted Carpaccio of Big Island Beef
SERVES 8

The 39th annual Kona Coffee Festival in 2009 was a jam-packed week of activity: parades, pageants, beauty contests, coffee tastings, entertainment, and, of course, the KTA Super Stores Kona Coffee Recipe Contest. The winner in the professional entrée division was Chef Morgan Starr of Mi's Italian Bistro in Kealakekua.

The winning dish was a carpaccio (thinly sliced, partially raw beef) seasoned with finely ground Kona coffee. Now you can make this at home! It's not all that difficult; you may spend more time shopping for this than you do cooking. If you can't find micro-greens (baby greens harvested while still young and tender), use your favorite salad greens. Truffle oil sounds expensive, but it is only flavored olive oil, and scarcely more expensive than any quality olive oil.

INGREDIENTS:
1 (1½ pound) Big Island beef tenderloin
¼ cup 100% Kona coffee, finely ground
Kona sea salt
Fresh-cracked black pepper
Olive oil for searing

For the salad:
8 ounces micro-greens
1 tablespoon extra-virgin olive oil
1 tablespoon lilikoi syrup
Salt and pepper to taste

For the garnish:
15 drops white truffle oil
2 ounces shaved cheese

PREPARATION:

To prepare the meat: Season the tenderloin with ground coffee, pepper, and salt. Heat a little olive oil in a large frying pan over medium high to high heat. You want the heat as high as it can go before the oil smokes. Sear the tenderloin on all sides until it is an even, rich brown all over. The inside will not be cooked; that's as it should be. Remove the beef from the pan and let it cool on a rack in the refrigerator. Once the meat is cold, wrap tightly it tightly in plastic wrap and freeze it. The meat may take about 2 hours to freeze.

(recipe continued on page 200)

To prepare the salad: Put the micro-greens or salad greens in a bowl and gently mix with the extra virgin olive oil, salt, pepper and lilikoi syrup.

Shave the Parmigiano-Reggiano cheese. If you have a cheese scraper, a girolle, you can use that, but a vegetable peeler will work too.

To cut the meat: Take the frozen tenderloin out of the freezer and cut it into slices as thin as you can manage. If it has frozen so hard that you cannot cut it, let it stand at room temperature for a few minutes and it will soften enough to cut.

PRESENTATION:

Arrange the thinly-sliced carpaccio on chilled plates, and garnish with salad, a few drops of of truffle oil, and shavings of cheese. Season with fresh cracked pepper and sea salt.

Memories of the Past

I remember restaurants: closed down, but favorite dishes aren't forgotten. Here are a few of those recipes.

I also remember mayors: Harry Kim, Steve Yamashiro, and Dante Carpenter. They shared some great recipes with me.

Grilled Shrimp Focaccia Club Sandwich
MAKES 4 SANDWICHES

Fiasco's was a great place for lunch, cocktails, and dinner. It was located on Kanoelehua Avenue, in Hilo. Their lunch sandwiches with criss-cross fries were always popular. Here is a recipe for their shrimp foccacia club sandwich. This dish makes a great brunch or light dinner.

INGREDIENTS:

20 (21–25 count) shrimp, peeled and deveined
Focaccia bread (enough to make one sandwich)
4 large lettuce leaves
½ cup sunflower sprouts
4 tomato slices, ¼-inch thick
8 slices of ripe avocado, ¼-inch thick
4 slices of sweet red onion, ¼-inch thick
4 slices of your favorite cheese
8 strips of cooked bacon

For the shrimp marinade:
1 cup olive oil
1 tablespoon minced garlic
1 tablespoon basil
1 teaspoon black pepper

For the pesto mayonnaise:
3 tablespoons mayonnaise
2 tablespoons basil pesto (see recipes on page 29 or 32, or use commercial pesto)

PREPARATION:

Combine the mayonnaise and the pesto to make pesto mayonnaise.

Mince the garlic for the marinade and combine all marinade ingredients.

Marinate the shrimp for 1 hour. Do not marinate any longer, as the shrimp will get soggy.

Lightly grill the shrimp, on a grill or in a grill pan, 2 minutes on each side.

To assemble sandwich: Split the focaccia bread and spread pesto mayonnaise on each side of bread. Arrange the grilled shrimps on the bread and add lettuce, sunflower sprouts, a tomato slice, sliced ripe avocado, red onion slices, cheese of your choice, and crispy bacon strips.

Pork Schnitzel
with Green Peppercorn Sauce
MAKES 6 CUTLETS

The Edelweiss restaurant opened in 1983 and quickly developed a devoted clientele. It was a great place for European food and many faithful patrons were sad when it closed its doors in November 2007.

Hans Peter Hager, the owner and chef, shared this recipe for pork schnitzel with green peppercorn sauce.

He uses the canned peppercorns because they're soaked in brine, and moist. Dry peppercorns would be too dry and hard.

INGREDIENTS:
6 pork loin cutlets (about 1½ pounds), cut ½-inch thick
1 beaten egg
2 tablespoons milk
¾ cup breadcrumbs
1 teaspoon paprika
¼ cup flour
1 teaspoon salt
½ teaspoon pepper
3 tablespoons olive oil

For the sauce:
1 teaspoon canned green peppercorns
1 tablespoon unsalted butter
4 tablespoons heavy cream

PREPARATION:

To prepare the sauce: Melt the butter in a small pan over medium heat. Add the green peppercorns and heavy cream and cook over low heat until thick.

To prepare the schnitzel: Whisk together the egg and 2 tablespoons milk in a bowl, and pour the mixture into a shallow baking pan. Mix bread crumbs and paprika together, place in another shallow baking pan. Mix flour, salt, and pepper together, place in yet another shallow baking pan. Line up the pans; this is your breading station.

Coat cutlets with flour and salt, then in egg mixture, and lastly in bread crumb mixture.

(recipe continued on page 204)

Heat the 3 tablespoons of olive oil in a large frying pan over medium high heat. Sauté the pork cutlets, turning once, until they are golden brown on each side.

PRESENTATION:
Arrange the cutlets on individual plates or a large serving platter, and top with green peppercorn sauce.

Oysters Bienville
SERVES 4 TO 6

Roussel's was a one-of-a-kind restaurant when it opened in Hilo town in 1985. Brothers Andrew and Spencer Oliver, along with a friend from their childhood days in Louisiana, Bert Roussel, turned a former bank into a classy New Orleans dining experience. We Hiloans got to dine on jambalaya, gumbo, shrimp creole, and soft-shell crab po' boys. We were so sad when the restaurant closed its doors.

Here is a great appetizer from Roussel's: oysters Bienville, oysters in a rich béchamel sauce. This classic New Orleans dish was named in honor of the city's founder, Jean-Baptiste le Moyne de Bienville.

Note that the sauce is to be cooked and then refrigerated for at least 2 hours before you bake the oysters. You might want to make it as much as a day ahead of time, if you are making this dish for a dinner party.

INGREDIENTS:
2 dozen oysters, on the half shell, drained
4 (9 x 13 baking pans) filled with rock salt to the depth of 1 inch

For the Bienville sauce:
1 cup shallots, finely chopped
¼ cup parsley, finely chopped
1½ teaspoon garlic, finely minced
4 large egg yolks, well beaten
½ cup (1 stick) butter
½ cup flour
½ cup heavy cream
1½ cups milk
¼ cup sherry
½ teaspoon cayenne
1 teaspoon salt
1 teaspoon white pepper, freshly ground

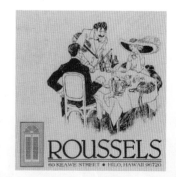

For the topping:
6 tablespoons Romano cheese, freshly-grated
4 tablespoons bread crumbs
½ teaspoon paprika
½ teaspoon salt

PREPARATION:

To prepare the topping: Put all ingredients in a blender. Blend at high speed for a few seconds, then turn the blender off and on, in short bursts, about 3 times. Put in a covered container and set aside.

TO PREPARE THE SAUCE:

Chop the shallots, parsley, and garlic per the instructions in the ingredients list. Separate the eggs and beat the yolks. Store the whites in the refrigerator to be used in another dish.

Put the butter in a large heavy saucepan and set over low heat. When the butter is melted, add the shallots, parsley, and garlic and cook, stirring frequently, until quite soft, about 10 minutes.

Gradually stir in the flour and mix with a wooden spoon until smooth. Add the cream and milk slowly, stirring or whisking constantly. The mixture should thicken, but stay smooth. Add a few spoonfuls of this mixture to the bowl of beaten egg yolk and whisk together. Pour the yolk mixture back into the saucepan, whisking as you pour. (You do this to reduce the chances that the yolks will lump, turning into scrambled eggs.) Add the sherry, cayenne, salt, and pepper, and mix thoroughly. Continue to cook over low heat for about 3 to 4 minutes, until the sauce is thick enough to coat the back of a spoon.

Spoon the sauce into a large, shallow porcelain or glass dish to a depth of 1½ to 2 inches. Let cool for a few minutes at room temperature, then cover with plastic wrap and refrigerate for at least 2 hours.

TO PREPARE THE OYSTERS:

Half an hour before you plan to bake the oysters, place the pans of rock salt in the oven and preheat the oven to 500°F.

Wash the oysters shells well, scrubbing with a brush if necessary; dry them thoroughly.

Put an oyster on each shell and set them, 6 to a pan, on the rock salt, spooning 1 heaping tablespoon of sauce evenly over each oyster. Sprinkle 1 level tablespoon of topping evenly over each sauced oyster. Bake for 15 to 18 minutes or until well browned on top. Serve hot.

'Ahi Soba Salad
SERVES 4 TO 6

Scruffles Restaurant was a family restaurant on Kīlauea Avenue. It is now an escrow office. Their chef, Henry Shiroma, is now working at the Kīlauea Military Camp in Volcano. This recipe was in Focus on Agriculture *by Jack Fujii.*

INGREDIENTS:

1 pound sashimi-grade Big Island 'ahi, cut into four (4 ounce) slices
½ cup purchased tempura sauce (Oriental section)
1 pound soba noodles
2 cups lettuce, cut into bite-sized pieces
½ cup red bell peppers, julienne
½ cup carrots, julienne
½ cup mung bean sprouts
½ cup sweet basil dressing (see recipe below)
½ cup won ton chips, for garnish

For the sweet basil dressing:
½ cup basil, fresh chopped
¼ cup onion, minced
1 clove garlic, peeled and trimmed
¾ cup honey
¼ cup corn syrup
¼ cup balsamic vinegar
¼ cup white vinegar
1 teaspoon dry mustard
1 teaspoon Worcestershire sauce
1 cup canola oil
½ tablespoon salt, or to taste
Black pepper, to taste

PREPARATION:

To make the dressing: Chop the basil and onions, peel and trim the garlic. Place the basil, onions, garlic, honey, corn syrup, vinegars, mustard, and Worcestershire sauce in a blender and purée. With the blender motor running, slowly pour the canola oil through the puka in the lid. This will emulsify the dressing. Add salt and pepper to taste.

Heat the tempura sauce in a sauté pan over medium heat. Add the 'ahi to the netsuke sauce and cook till just cooked through. Do not overcook.

Bring a pot of water to boil, add the soba noodles, boil till tender, drain and rinse under cold running water. Set aside.

(recipe continued on page 208)

Cut up the lettuce, bell peppers, and carrots per the instructions in the ingredient list.

PRESENTATION:

Put the lettuce, bell peppers, carrots, and bean sprouts in a large salad bowl. Top with the soba noodles, cooked 'ahi, and won ton chips. Drizzle dressing over the salad.

Spicy Tofu Spread for Sandwiches
MAKES 1 CUP

I loved the spicy tofu sandwich from O'Keefe's and Sons, Bread Bakers. This downtown Hilo bakery was the best place to buy sandwiches.

INGREDIENTS:
    1 block (12 ounces) firm tofu
    5 ounces frozen peas
    1 teaspoon ginger, grated
    1 teaspoon garlic, pressed
    1 tablespoon soy sauce
    2 tablespoons Thai yellow curry paste
    1 teaspoon sesame oil

PREPARATION:

Pat and dry tofu, then coarsely grate it. Cook the frozen peas, in a small pan of boiling water on the stove or in a few inches of water in the microwave; drain. Peel and grate the ginger; peel the garlic and put it through a garlic press.

Put the ginger, garlic, soy sauce, Thai yellow curry paste, and sesame oil in bowl and mix well. Gently fold in the tofu and the cooked, cooled peas.

Serve on hearty sandwich bread or whole-wheat pita pocket bread.

Peanut Butter Sauce
MAKES 1 CUP

Steven Yamashiro, who was mayor of the County of Hawai'i from 1993 to 2000, likes peanut butter sauce as made by his wife Della. This sauce is wonderful with baked chicken, blanched vegetables, or tofu.

INGREDIENTS:

- ½ cup daikon, finely grated
- 1 garlic clove
- ¼ cup peanut butter
- 1 tablespoon skim milk powder
- ¼ teaspoon honey
- 2 tablespoons lemon juice
- 2 tablespoons soy sauce

PREPARATION:

Peel and grate the daikon. Peel the garlic, chop it, and put it through a garlic press.

Mix all ingredients thoroughly; the sauce should have the consistency of heavy cream. If you like smoother sauce, blend the mixture in a blender or with a stick blender.

Serve over hot or cold tofu, blanched vegetables, roasted chicken breast, or as a cracker dip.

Liliko'i Cheesecake

In the early '90s, Kay Cabrera opened up Kay's Creations in Waiākea Village, along the banks of the Wailoa River. It was a wonderful place to satisfy your sweet tooth. She stocked pies, tarts, cakes, and cheesecakes.

Now Kay and her husband Kevin make fabulous artisan breads and sell them at the Parker School Farmers' Market, Saturdays in Kamuela. I love the bread, and I suppose it's healthier than the sweets, but oh, I miss the sweets.

At least I can make my own liliko'i cheesecake, thanks to Kay, who was willing to share the recipe. I use my own homemade liliko'i purée (so easy to make; stored in bags in the freezer), but you can use frozen juice from the supermarket too.

INGREDIENTS:

For the topping:
½ cup lilikoi purée OR passion fruit juice concentrate
½ cup sugar
½ cup water
1½ teaspoon unflavored gelatin, softened in 2 tablespoons cold water

For the crust:
1 cup almonds, slivered and blanched
2 ounces (¼ stick) butter
⅛ teaspoon (a pinch) salt
2 tablespoons sugar
2 ounces bittersweet chocolate, cut up

For the filling:
1 tablespoon unflavored gelatin, softened in 3 tablespoons of cold water
2 (8 ounce) packages cream cheese, softened at room temperature
¾ cup sugar
1 teaspoon vanilla extract
½ cup lilikoi purée
1 cup heavy cream

PREPARATION:

To prepare the topping: Bring the purée, sugar and water to a boil. Remove from heat and add the softened gelatin. Stir until dissolved. Pass through fine mesh strainer into a heat proof measuring cup and cool to room temperature, stirring once or twice to prevent a skin from forming. (If you're careful to mix

(recipe continued on page 212)

MEMORIES OF THE PAST   211 thoroughly, you might be able to skip the step with the sieve. If you're worried about lumps in the topping, use the sieve.)

To prepare the crust: Toast the almonds at 350°F until golden and fragrant. While hot, add them to the bowl of food processor with the remaining crust ingredients and grind until fine. Press into the bottom of a 9-inch spring form pan. Refrigerate to cool and set while you make the filling.

To prepare the filling: Dissolve the gelatin in the cold water. Set aside. Cream the cheese and sugar in bowl of food processor until no lumps remain. Pour vanilla, lilikoi purée, and dissolved gelatin through the feed tube while machine is still running, scraping once or twice, blending until smooth.

Whip the cream in a separate bowl until soft peaks form. Fold the whipped cream into the lilikoi mixture.Scrape the mixture into the crust lined pan and refrigerate until set (or freeze for 30 minutes). When cheesecake is set, carefully pour the cooled topped topping over the surface. Chill several hours or overnight.

To serve, carefully run an offset spatula around the pan to release the sides. Remove the ring. Use the offset spatula to run carefully under the crust to loosen then slide the cheesecake onto a serving platter.

Ono Lemon Piccata
SERVES 2

It was always entertaining to visit the old Topo Gigio's restaurant. The owner, Perry Poli-cicchio, had a fabulous toy collection that he displayed in the dining room. An old red wagon hung from the rafters. Model planes and dolls brought back many pleasant child-hood memories.

The food was good too. Here is one of my favorites, a fish and lemon dish.

INGREDIENTS:
¼ cup white button mushrooms, sliced (¼-inch slices)
1 tablespoon garlic, minced
¼ cup olive oil
1 pound fresh ono fillets
¼ cup flour
2 tablespoons capers
1 teaspoon garlic salt
1 teaspoon black pepper
2 tablespoons lemon juice (about 1 lemon)
¼ cup white wine

PREPARATION:

Clean and slice the mushrooms; peel and mince the garlic.

Put the olive oil in a large sauté pan over medium high heat. Flour the ono fillets and sauté in the hot oil for about 3 minutes. The fish should not be completely cooked. If it is, then it will be overcooked after you finish cooking the rest of the ingredients.

Add the mushrooms, garlic, capers, salt and pepper and cook until the mushrooms wilt. Add the wine and lemon juice. Add a pinch of flour, sprinkling it over the top of the pan and mixing as you sprinkle. This reduces the chance that the flour will lump.

PRESENTATION:

Serve over buttered pasta or rice.

Ugly Duckling Cake
MAKES ONE 13 x 9 INCH CAKE

Harry Kim was the Hawai'i County mayor from 2000 to 2008. He was not your usual politician. Before he ran for mayor, he was our county director of civil defense for sixteen years, warning us when volcanoes and tsunamis threatened. When he campaigned, he refused any donations over $10. When he became mayor, he wore jeans to work every day.

This is Harry's favorite cake. He first ate it at a picnic, twenty-five years ago, and was so pleased that his wife, Bobbie, made a point of getting the recipe. Now she makes it for him on special occasions, like his birthday.

INGREDIENTS:
    1 (18.25 ounce) Betty Crocker Super Moist yellow cake mix
    1 (16 ounce) can fruit cocktail
    2 large eggs
    ¼ cup canola or vegetable oil
    ½ cup angel flake coconut
    ½ cup brown sugar

    For the topping:
    ½ cup butter
    ½ cup sugar
    ½ cup evaporated milk
    ½ cup angel flake coconut

PREPARATION:

Preheat oven to 325°F. Lightly spray or grease a 13 x 9 inch pan, bottom only.

Blend the cake mix, fruit cocktail, eggs, and oil in your mixer bowl. Add coconut and beat for 2 minutes at medium speed. Pour into the prepared pan. Sprinkle brown sugar over the cake mixture. Bake at 325°F for 45 minutes, or until a toothpick inserted in the cake comes out clean. Let the cake cool, in the pan, while you prepare the topping.

Put the butter, sugar, and evaporated milk in a small saucepan over medium heat. Bring the mixture to a boil, stirring constantly. Boil and stir for 2 minutes. Remove the pan from the heat and add the coconut. Slowly spoon the hot mxiture over the warm cake.

You can serve the cake while it is still warm, or wait until it has cooled.

Pot Roast Pork
SERVES 10

Herbert Matayoshi was the mayor of the County of Hawai'i from 1977 to 1985. His wife Mary and her sister have dinner together once a week. They often make this easy and delicious pork dish.

INGREDIENTS:
    5 pounds pork butt
    1 clove garlic
    1-inch piece of ginger
    1 tablespoon canola oil, for browning the meat
    ⅓ cup sugar
    ⅓ cup white vinegar
    ½ cup soy sauce
    1 cup water
    1 cup chicken broth
    3 medium carrots, cut into 2-inch chunks
    3 russet potatoes, peeled and cut into 2-inch cubes and chunks
    2 round onions, cut into 2-inch chunks

For the cornstarch slurry (optional):
    2 tablespoons cornstarch
    4 tablespoons cold water

PREPARATION:

You can leave the pork butt whole, or you can cut it into 2-inch cubes for faster cooking. Peel the garlic and the ginger; smash with the flat side of a heavy kitchen knife. You will probably want to remove them from the gravy before serving.

Put 1 tablespoon of canola oil in a large stock pot over a medium flame. Brown the pork on all sides, turning as necessary. If you have cut up the pork, the drippings from the pork pieces will probably be enough to finish cooking the meat. If you are cooking a whole butt, you may have to add a little more oil. When the pork is browned, add the garlic and ginger and cook a little longer.

Add the sugar, vinegar, soy sauce, water and chicken broth and simmer for 2 hours or until the meat is tender. If you cut up the meat, it will probably cook faster. Check the pot occasionally to stir and test for tenderness.

While the pork is simmering, cut up the carrots, potatoes, and onions per the instructions in the ingredients list.

(recipe continued on page 216)

Add vegetables and continue simmering until the vegetables are tender. This may take about 30 to 40 minutes.

If you like a thicker gravy, mix up the cornstarch slurry. Stir 2 tablespoons cornstarch into 4 tablespoons cold water, until you have a smooth paste. Add to the pot and stir as the gravy thickens.

Some 'Ono Clam Chowder Li' Dat
SERVES 6

Dante Carpenter was the mayor of the County of Hawai'i from 1985 till 1988. He and his wife Olan raised their four children in Ka'ū and Hilo; now they have retired and live on O'ahu.

Olan is the cook in the family. She likes to make this easy clam chowder, one of Dante's favorites.

INGREDIENTS:
½ to 1 round onion, cut into ½-inch chunks
3 stalks celery, cut into ½-inch chunks
3 medium russet potatoes, peeled and cut into ½-inch chunks
¼ pound bacon, cut into ½-inch long pieces
1 (13 ounce) can evaporated milk
1 (6½ ounce) can chopped or minced clams
1 (15¼ ounce) can corn kernels
2 to 4 tablespoons instant mashed potatoes, as thickening (optional)

PREPARATION:

Chop the onion, celery, potatoes, and bacon per the instructions in the ingredients list.

Sauté the bacon pieces in a large pot over medium heat. When they are almost cooked, pour off most of the oil; leave about 2 tablespoons or so. Add the onions and celery and finish cooking the bacon and vegetables together. Add the canned milk and diced potatoes. Add 2 cans of water; you can use the empty evaporated milk can to measure it. Add the canned clams and corn; don't drain them, add the juices too. Simmer the chowder until the potatoes are tender. Season with salt and pepper. If you like a thick chowder, add some or all of the instant mashed potatoes to thicken.

Omiyage Sweets

When local visitors come to the Big Island, they leave with omiyage. Often enough, the omiyage are sweet. Visitors head for Big Island Candies, for chocolate-covered shortbread, and Two Ladies Kitchen, for mochi.

Not all the great cooks are commercial. In kitchens across the island, talented men and women are making sweets that wow their families, their guests, and anyone lucky enough to attend a potluck or backyard lū'au that features these luscious concoctions. I've collected a few of those recipes, too. Do try a few of these time-tested treats!

Irma Ikawa's Haupia Squares
MAKES 24 PIECES

Big Island Candies has been making and selling high-quality macadamia nut candies and cookies since 1977. They believe in using 100% Hawaiʻi-grown macadamia nuts and Kona coffee, Island eggs, real butter, and high-grade chocolate. They don't cut corners. Their customers know and taste the difference—that's why the shop wins awards and that's why it does such a thriving business in omiyage.

Owners Alan and Irma Ikawa were willing to share the recipe for their favorite dessert.

INGREDIENTS:

For the crust:
4 tablespoons powdered sugar
1½ cups white all-purpose flour
¾ cup Big Island macadamia nuts, chopped
¾ cup (1½ sticks) butter

For the filling:
2 (14 ounce) cans coconut milk
¾ cup sugar
1 cup water
7 tablespoons cornstarch mixed with ½ cup cold water

For the topping:
1 (8 ounce) container of frozen whipped topping, thawed

PREPARATION:

Preheat oven to 350°F.

To prepare the crust: Mix the sugar, flour, and chopped nuts. Cut the butter into small pieces and work it into the dry ingredients as if you were making pie crust. Some people like to do this with two knives or a pastry cutter; some people do it with their fingers. It's up to you. Press the crust mixture into a 9 x 13 inch baking pan. Bake at 350°F for 20 minutes, or until slightly brown around the edges.

To prepare the filling: Put the coconut milk, sugar, and water in a saucepan over medium heat. Mix the cornstarch and cold water and add to the coconut mixture. Cook until the mixture boils and thickens, stirring frequently. If the mixture is grainy, keep cooking; the fat in the coconut hasn't melted yet. When the mixture is thick and smooth, remove from heat and cool to lukewarm. Pour the haupia mixture over the baked crust. Chill for 3 to 4 hours.

When thoroughly chilled, spread the whipped topping over the haupia. Cut the haupia into 24 squares.

Betsy Mitchell's Best Ever Cookies
MAKES 8 DOZEN COOKIES

Betsy Mitchell is the honorary mayor of Volcano, where she has lived since 1982. Before she retired, she headed the Blood Bank of Hawai'i. Now that she's officially retired, she seems to be as busy as ever, working for the Volcano community and serving as the Volcano district police commissioner.

She is also known for her chocolate chip cookies, which frequently feature at bake sales, pot-lucks, and community celebrations. The secret ingredient? All is revealed: it's cornflakes!

INGREDIENTS:
- 1 cup butter (2 sticks)
- 1 cup white sugar
- 1 cup brown sugar, packed
- 1 large egg
- 1 cup canola oil
- 1 teaspoon salt
- 1 teaspoon vanilla extract
- 1 teaspoon baking soda
- 1 cup rolled oats
- 1 cup crushed corn flakes
- 5 cups flour
- 1 (12 ounce) package chocolate chips
- ⅔ cup walnuts, chopped

PREPARATION:

Preheat oven to 300°F.

Add to your food processor or mixer bowl: butter, white sugar, brown sugar, egg, oil, salt, vanilla and baking soda. Mix well. You'll have a smooth paste.

In another bowl, gently mix the oats, flour, cornflakes, chips, and nuts.

Gently combine the butter-sugar mixture and the bowl of oat-flakes-nuts. You should probably do this with a spatula, so that the chunky goodies stay crisp and separate.

Drop rounded teaspoonfuls of dough on a cookie sheet lined with parchment paper, about 1 inch apart, and flatten with a fork dipped in water. Bake until light brown, or about 20 minutes.

Layered Manju
MAKES 24 PIECES

Haunani Ogata is an adopted Hiloan. She was born and raised on O'ahu, but she married a Hilo boy, Wesley Ogata. She works at the Hawai'i Tribune Herald, where she is known for her friendly ways and her layered manju. This is a super easy recipe because it's made in a pan, like bar cookies, rather than formed into individual manju. Same great taste, half the work!

INGREDIENTS:
- 1 large egg
- 5 cups unsifted white all-purpose flour
- ½ cup sugar
- ½ teaspoon salt
- 2 cups (4 sticks) butter
- ¾ cup condensed milk
- 2 (14.11 ounce) bags koshi-an

PREPARATION:

Preheat the oven to 375°F.

Beat the egg in a small bowl and set it aside.

Whisk together the flour, sugar, and salt in a large bowl. With a spoon or your mixer, cream the butter. Add the dry ingredients and the sweetened condensed milk to the butter. First a little dry mixture, mix, then a little milk, mix, dry mixture, mix, and so on. Don't add them all at once.

Divide the dough into two equal parts. Spread one half of the dough into the bottom of a 9 x 13 inch baking pan. Make sure that you fill the corners and level the dough. Spread koshi-an over the dough. Spread the remaining dough on top of the koshi-an. Press to fill the corners and level the dough. Brush the beaten egg over the top of the dough.

Bake at 375°F for 40 to 45 minutes.

Kathy's Custard Pie
MAKES ONE 10-INCH PIE

Kathy Higaki, the business manager for the Hawai'i Tribune-Herald, *is known for her pies. Friends beg her to bring pies for Thanksgiving and other special occasions. Now you can make some of her special treats at home.*

INGREDIENTS:

4 large eggs
½ cup sugar
¼ teaspoon salt
1 teaspoon vanilla extract
2½ cups milk
1 (10-inch) pre-cooked pie crust (see below)

For the crust:
2 cups flour
1 teaspoon salt
¾ cup vegetable shortening
¼ cup ice water

This recipe makes 2 (10-inch) crusts. Use one for the custard pie and put the other in the freezer, to be used later, perhaps for Kathy's Peanut Butter Cream Pie (see page 225).

PREPARATION:

To prepare the crust: Sift together the flour and salt. Add shortening, cutting it into the flour with a pastry blender. The mixture should form small balls the size of green peas. Add the ice water a little at a time, mixing with a fork till it comes together and forms a ball.

Pinch the dough in half. Roll out one of the halves on floured waxed paper or a silpat pastry mat. Don't roll the dough more than once. If the dough tears, pinch it together with your fingers rather than gathering it up and rerolling. If you work the dough too much, it will become tough and heavy.

Roll the dough around the rolling pin to transfer it to the pie pan. Unroll it into the pan. Gather up the edges and pinch them between your fingers to form an even ridge around the edge of the pie pan. You can decoratively flute the ridge by pinching it between your thumb and forefinger, or you can use a fork to push it down into tiny ridges.

You can freeze the other half of the dough in a zip-lock plastic bag. It can be thawed and rolled out when needed.

Chill the unbaked pie crust for ½ hour. This keeps it from slipping down the sides of the pan when baking. While it is chilling, preheat your oven to 350°F.

Line the bottom of the crust with parchment paper or aluminum foil. Fill the pan ⅔ full with dried beans, rice, or pie weights. These prevent the dough from puffing up unevenly.

Bake with the weights in the crust for 20 minutes. Remove the crust from the oven, cool a few minutes and carefully remove the pie weights. Use a fork to poke small holes in the bottom of the pie crust and return the crust to the oven (without the weights). Cook for an additional 10 minutes, until the crust is golden. Cool completely before filling.

TO PREPARE THE FILLING:

Preheat the oven to 475°F.

Beat the eggs in your mixer or with a whisk; mix in the sugar, salt, and vanilla. Scald the milk. Pour the hot milk slowly into the egg mixture, whisking or mixing as you pour. Pour the custard into the pre-baked pie shell; sprinkle ¼ teaspoon ground cinnamon over the top, if you'd like, for a bit of extra flavor and a color accent.

Bake the pie in the pre-heated 475°F oven for 5 minutes, reduce heat to 425°F and bake for another 10 to 15 minutes, or until a knife inserted in center of pie comes out clean.

Cool at room temperature and, if possible, serve within 3 hours. If the pie is to be left out any longer than 3 hours, it must be refrigerated. Custards often "weep" moisture under refrigeration, so a chilled pie may not be as good as one eaten immediately after baking.

Kathy's Peanut Butter Cream Pie
MAKES ONE 10-INCH PIE

Here's another spectacular pie from Kathy Higaki that will disappear in the blink of an eye.

INGREDIENTS:

1 (10-inch) baked and cooled pie shell (see the instructions on page 222)

For the crumb topping:
¾ cup powdered sugar, sifted
½ cup creamy peanut butter (Jif preferred)

For the cream filling:
½ cup sugar
3 tablespoons cornstarch, packed, not loose
½ teaspoon salt
3 egg yolks, slightly beaten
2½ cups milk
2 teaspoons vanilla extract

For the meringue topping:
3 egg whites
¼ teaspoon cream of tartar
6 tablespoons sugar

PREPARATION:

Preheat oven to 425°F.

To prepare the crumb topping: Combine powdered sugar and peanut butter till mixture resembles coarse crumbs. Reserve 4 tablespoons of the crumb mixture for the top of the meringue and sprinkle the remaining crumb mixture in the bottom of the baked pie shell. Set aside.

To prepare the filling: Whisk together the sugar, cornstarch, and salt. Pour the egg yolks and milk into a medium-size saucepan and mix well. Stir in the sugar-cornstarch mixture and mix again. Cook the mixture over medium heat, stirring constantly, until the mixture comes to a boil. Continue to stir and boil for 1 to 2 minutes. Remove the pan from the heat and stir in the vanilla. Cool to room temperature and pour into the pre-baked pie shell.

To prepare the meringue: Beat the egg whites till a soft foam forms. Add ¼ teaspoon cream of tartar, then gradually add sugar, 1 tablespoon at a time, beating at high speed until the meringue forms stiff peaks.

(recipe continued on page 226)

To assemble the pie: Spread the meringue mixture over the filling. Make sure that the meringe goes right up to the crust; if it is left to float on top of the filling, it will shrink during baking. Sprinkle the reserved peanut butter topping crumbs over the meringue.

Bake at 425°F for 10 to 15 minutes, or until the meringue is lightly browned. Cool to room temperature before serving. Do not leave this pie out at room temperature more than 3 hours; refrigerate it after that, to prevent spoilage.

Avocado Cream Cheese Squares
MAKES 24 (2 X 2 INCH) SQUARES

My friend Sylvia Dixon makes this special dessert every time she has visitors, and each time she makes it, her guests love it!

INGREDIENTS:

For the first layer:
2 cups flour
¼ cup sugar
1 cup (2 sticks) butter

For the second layer:
1 (3 ounce) box lime gelatin
1 cup hot water
8 ounces cream cheese, softened at room temperature
½ cup sugar
8 ounces frozen whipped topping

For the third layer:
2 (3 ounce) boxes or 1 large (6 ounce) box lime gelatin
1 (.25 ounce) envelope unflavored gelatin
½ cup sugar
2 cups hot water
2 cups ripe avocado, mashed
½ cup mayonnaise
½ cup milk

PREPARATION:

Preheat oven to 350°F.

To make the first layer: Whisk together the flour and sugar. Cut the butter into the flour-sugar mix with a pastry blender or two knives. You will end up with a

(recipe continued on page 228)

crumbly dough. Pat the dough into an even layer in a 9 x 13 inch baking pan. Bake for 20 to 30 minutes or until a light golden brown.

To make the second layer: Mix the lime gelatin, unflavored gelatin and hot water in a small bowl. Stir until all the gelatin is dissolved. Set the mixture aside to cool completely. Put the cream cheese and ½ cup sugar into your mixer bowl and whip to cream. Fold in the thawed whipped topping. Pour the cooled lime gelatin into the mixer bowl and fold it into the cream cheese mixture. Pour this mixture over the cooled crust and refrigerate until very firm.

To make the third layer: Mix lime gelatin, unflavored gelatin, sugar and hot water in a small bowl. Set aside to cool completely. Peel, pit, and mash the avocado. Put the avocado, mayonnaise, and milk in a food processor or blender and purée. Add the cooled gelatin mixture to the processor or blender and mix again. Spoon mixture over the previous two layers. Spread evenly and refrigerate overnight.

Cut into squares before serving. (Cut into 4 (13-inch) strips the long way, then cut across 6 times. You'll get 24 squares, each slightly larger than 2 x 2 inches.)

Roulade au Citron (Lemon Roll)
MAKES ONE 10 x 6 ROLL, SERVING 8

Richard Myers loves to cook and garden. This dessert is a favorite. He says it is worth the effort.

INGREDIENTS:

For the Curd/Filling:
2 sticks unsalted butter (1 cup)
⅔ cup sugar
4 egg yolks
¼ cup each lemon juice and water
1 teaspoon Grand Marnier
¼ teaspoon lemon peel, grated

For the Sponge Cake:
4 eggs, separated
¼ cup sugar
¼ teaspoon of cream of tartar
¼ cup flour
¼ cup cornstarch
1 teaspoon vanilla extract
½ teaspoon lemon peel, grated

OMIYAGE SWEETS

Garnish:
1 cup whipping cream
¼ cup sugar
1 teaspoon Grand Marnier liqueur

TO PREPARE THE FILLING:

Beat the egg yolks and sugar until light yellow. Pour the egg yolks into a heavy pan. Add butter, lemon juice and water. Cook over low heat, stirring constantly, until mixture coats the spoon or about 10 minutes. Remove from heat and add lemon peel and Grand Marnier. Cover surface with wax paper (so a skin does not form on the surface) and chill for several hours.

TO PREPARE THE SPONGE CAKE:

Pre heat the oven to 400°F. Butter a 10 x 15 jelly roll pan and line it with wax paper which is then buttered.

Separate the eggs. Put the egg whites and cream of tartar into the bowl of your electric mixer and whip until soft peaks form. Add sugar and continue whipping until stiff peaks form.

In another bowl beat egg yolks until they are pale yellow. Add ¼ of egg whites and gently fold the egg whites into the yolks. Add remaining whites into yolks and carefully fold to blend. Add vanilla extract and grated lemon peel.

Pour batter into prepared pan and smooth with spatula to even the batter. Bake for 10 minutes in the 400°F oven—do not overbake.

Invert the jelly roll pan over a cookie sheet dusted with powdered sugar. The cake will fall out of the baking pan onto the sheet with the wax paper still attached to the bottom. Allow the cake to stand and cool completely before you carefully loosen the edges of the wax paper to peel off. (If you aren't careful you'll pull away chunks of cake and your roll will look ragged.)

TO ASSEMBLE:

Spread the chilled filling over the cake. Whip the whipping cream until stiff. Add sugar and Grand Marnier. Spread the flavored cream over the lemon filling.

Carefully roll up the entire cake. Place on a serving platter, seam side down. Dust with powdered sugar.

Save any leftover filling or whipped cream and use them to garnish servings of the lemon roll.

Poi Andagi
MAKES 60 DOUGHNUT BALLS

Kaua'i is the taro-growing champ of the Islands, but the Big Island also has thriving taro and poi industries. Use some of our great local poi to make these delicious Okinawan andagi, or doughnuts.

INGREDIENTS:
- **6 cups flour**
- **3 cups sugar**
- **5 teaspoons baking powder**
- **3 eggs**
- **3 cups poi**
- **½ cup milk**
- **Canola oil for deep frying**

PREPARATION:

Sift or whisk together the flour, sugar, and baking powder. Beat the eggs and mix them with the poi and milk. Add the flour mixture, ⅓ at a time, to the liquid ingredients, beating after each addition. The dough should be stiff and not too soft.

If you have a deep-fryer, heat the oil to 325°F and drop golf-ball-size fistfuls or spoonfuls of andagi into the oil. Do not crowd the oil; this lowers the heat and makes the andagi greasy. Cook, turning frequently, until the andagi are golden-brown all over. Remove and drain on paper towels.

If you don't have a deep fryer, heat at least 2 inches of oil in deep frying pan to 325°F. Cook as above.

Kathy's Cinnamon Rolls
MAKES 8 ROLLS

Many cinnamon roll recipes call for yeast dough, which requires expert handling and a long rising time. Kathy Higaki makes delicious baking-powder cinnamon rolls that can be made in less than an hour. Try them some morning when you want to treat yourself!

INGREDIENTS:
- 2 cups flour
- 1 tablespoon baking powder
- ½ teaspoon salt
- 6 to 7 tablespoons vegetable shortening
- ½ cup milk
- ½ cup sugar
- 2 tablespoons ground cinnamon
- ¼ cup (½ stick) butter

PREPARATION:
Preheat oven to 450°F.

Sift the flour, baking powder, and salt together. Cut the shortening into the dry ingredients with a pastry blender, two knives, or your fingers. You should have a crumbly mixture that looks like coarse cornmeal.

Add milk to form a soft dough, like biscuit dough. Roll out the dough on a floured surface and shape into a 8 x 10 inch rectangle.

Mix the sugar and ground cinnamon in a small bowl.

Place the butter in a 2-cup glass measuring cup and soften it in your microwave oven. Heat it in small bursts and check after each burst. It should be soft, not melted.

Use a spoon or offset spatula to spread the softened butter over the rectangle of dough. Sprinkle the cinnamon-sugar mixture evenly over the butter. Roll up the dough, starting with one of the long sides. Cut the roll into slices 1½-inch wide. Place the rolls, cut side down, on an ungreased cookie sheet.

Bake in the pre-heated 450°F oven for 10 to 15 minutes or until done.

Index

flour, bread 120, 150, 187
flour, cake 172
flour, rice 166
fruit cocktail 214
Fujii, Jack 207
furikake 33-34, 125-126

G

garbanzo beans 88-89
gelatin 98, 128, 211-212, 226, 228
ginger, powdered 60
Glow Hawai'i 66
gobo (burdock root) 24-25
Gomes, George 190
Grand Marnier liqueur 229
Grand Passion liqueur 190
Green Goose Gourmet 123
green peas 8, 130, 137, 222
green tea powder 98

H

half-and-half 165
ham 156, 197
ham, prosciutto 197
Hawai'i Community College 150
Hawai'i Island Home for Recovery 147
Hawaiian chili pepper 38, 66, 78, 94
Hawaiian sea salt 69
heavy cream 30-31, 104, 192, 203-204, 209, 211
Hilo Coffee Mill 108
Hilo Hawaiian Hotel 44, 116
Hilo High School 96, 137, 152
Hilo Medical Center 145, 151
Hilo Yacht Club 75, 131
Hilo's Seaside Restaurant 33
hō'i'o fern shoot 66
hoisin sauce 6
hondashi 106-107
honey 2, 76, 125, 187, 190, 197, 207, 209
hot sauce 22, 128, 197

I

Island Naturals Market and Deli 32

J

jalapeño pepper 43, 103

K

Kaffir lime leaf 178
Kahua Ranch 79, 85, 91-92
Kailua Candy Company 30
Kay's Creations 211
Keauhou Beach Hotel 192
Kenney, Ed 86
Kenoi, Billy 96, 158
Keosavang, Thepthikona "TK" 68
ketchup 92, 108, 147, 155
kidney beans 151
kim chee 17-18, 118
Kim, Harry 201, 214
kochujahng (spicy Korean sauce) 127
Kodama, D.K. 175
kombu 69-70, 172
Kona Brewing Company 109
Kona Cold Lobster 76
Kona Inn Restaurant 165
Kona Village Resort 99, 187
konnyaku (yam cake) 106-107
koshi-an (bean paste) 188, 221
KTA Super Stores 1-3, 8, 11, 13, 17, 27, 103, 114, 118, 199
Kuahiwi Ranch 81
Kuhio Grille 189
Kurisu, Derek 3

L

lamb 79, 91-93, 161, 189
lamb leg 91
lamb shoulder 92
Lamb, Mike 161
Leilani Bakery 35
lemon 38, 47-48, 56-57, 64, 66, 68-69,

About the Author

Audrey Wilson is a food columnist, cooking instructor, and is the author of three locally-published cookbooks: *What the Big Island Likes to Eat* (2008), *A Mother's Gift to Her Three Sons* (2007) and *An Eruption of Recipes from Volcano* (2002).

She writes a weekly column for the *Hawaii Tribune Herald* called "Let's Talk Food," and has taught cooking classes at Ke Anuenue Area Health Center, Hilo Adult Education, and several Big Island senior centers.

Wilson has traveled the world with her husband and has taken cooking classes in such places as: Paris, France; Sorrento, Italy; Florence, Italy; Chiang Mai, Thailand; Costa Brava, Spain; and New Orleans, Louisiana.

Wilson graduated from Hilo High School and received a BS in Home Economics from the University of Hawai'i at Mānoa. She and her husband, Jim Wilson, Publisher Emeritus of the *Hawaii Tribune Herald*, live in Volcano. There they preside over AJ's Volcano Cottage, a two unit bed and breakfast, and AJ's Volcano Cooking School.

Also by Audrey Wilson

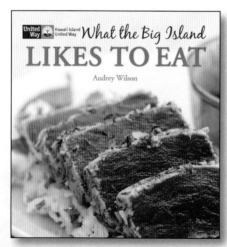

What the Big Island Likes to Eat

The quest always asked of Big Island residents, both when they travel as well as by visitors to the island—is "what do you like to eat?" The answer: food from all over—food that was once Polynesian, Asian, European or American. We mix 'em up, give 'em a local twist, and enjoy. Contains over 125 recipes.

ISBN-10: 1-56647-886-3
ISBN-13: 978-1-56647-886-1
Trim size: 9 x 9 in. • Page count: 224 pp
Binding: Hardcover • Retail: $31.95

To order, visit:
www.mutualpublishing.com